CONTENTS

▶ Unit 1: ADDITION AND SUBTRACTION CONCEPTS

▶ Chapter 1: Addition Concepts
1.1 Model Addition Stories **1**
1.2 Use Symbols to Add **2**
1.3 Algebra: Add 0 . . . . **3**
1.4 Problem Solving • Write a
    Number Sentence **4**

▶ Chapter 2: Using Addition
2.1 Algebra: Add in Any Order **5**
2.2 Ways to Make 7 and 8 . . . . **6**
2.3 Ways to Make 9 and 10 . . . . **7**
2.4 Vertical Addition **8**
2.5 Problem Solving • Make a Model . . . **9**

▶ Chapter 3: Subtraction Concepts
3.1 Model Subtraction Stories **10**
3.2 Use Symbols to Subtract **11**
3.3 Algebra: Write Subtraction
    Sentences **12**
3.4 Problem Solving • Make a Model . . . **13**
3.5 Algebra: Subtract All or Zero **14**

▶ Chapter 4: Using Subtraction
4.1 Take Apart 7 and 8 . . . . **15**
4.2 Take Apart 9 and 10 . . . . **16**
4.3 Vertical Subtraction **17**
4.4 Subtract to Compare **18**
4.5 Problem Solving • Draw a Picture . . **19**

▶ Unit 2: ADDITION AND SUBTRACTION FACTS TO 10

▶ Chapter 5: Addition Strategies
5.1 Count On 1 and 2 . . . . **20**
5.2 Use a Number Line to Count On . . **21**
5.3 Use Doubles **22**
5.4 Problem Solving • Draw a Picture . . **23**

▶ Chapter 6: Addition Facts Practice
6.1 Use the Strategies **24**
6.2 Sums to 8 . . . . **25**
6.3 Sums to 10 . . . . **26**
6.4 Algebra: Follow the Rule **27**
6.5 Problem Solving • Write a
    Number Sentence **28**

▶ Chapter 7: Subtraction Strategies
7.1 Use a Number Line to Count
    Back 1 and 2 . . . . **29**
7.2 Use a Number Line to Count
    Back 3 . . . . **30**
7.3 Algebra: Relate Addition and
    Subtraction **31**
7.4 Problem Solving • Draw a Picture . . **32**

▶ Chapter 8: Subtraction Facts Practice
8.1 Use the Strategies **33**
8.2 Subtraction to 10 . . . . **34**
8.3 Algebra: Follow the Rule **35**
8.4 Fact Families to 10 . . . . **36**
8.5 Problem Solving • Choose the
    Operation **37**

▶ **Unit 3: GRAPHS, NUMBERS TO 100, AND FACTS TO 12**

▶ **Chapter 9: Graphs and Tables**

9.1 Algebra: Sort and Classify **38**

9.2 Make Concrete Graphs **39**

9.3 Make Picture Graphs **40**

9.4 Read a Tally Table **41**

9.5 Make Bar Graphs **42**

9.6 Problem Solving • Use Data from a Graph **43**

9.7 Interpret Graphs **44**

▶ **Chapter 10: Place Value to 100**

10.1 Teen Numbers **45**

10.2 Tens **46**

10.3 Tens and Ones to 50 . . . . **47**

10.4 Tens and Ones to 100 . . . . **48**

10.5 Algebra: Different Ways to Make Numbers **49**

10.6 Problem Solving • Make Reasonable Estimates **50**

▶ **Chapter 11: Comparing and Ordering Numbers**

11.1 Algebra: Greater Than **51**

11.2 Algebra: Less Than **52**

11.3 Algebra: Use Symbols to Compare **53**

11.4 Order on a Number Line **54**

11.5 Count Forward and Backward **55**

11.6 Problem Solving • Use a Model . . **56**

▶ **Chapter 12: Number Patterns**

12.1 Skip Count by 2s, 5s, and 10s **57**

12.2 Algebra: Use a Hundred Chart to Skip Count **58**

12.3 Algebra: Patterns on a Hundred Chart **59**

12.4 Even and Odd **60**

12.5 Problem Solving • Find a Pattern . . **61**

12.6 Ordinal Numbers **62**

▶ **Chapter 13: Addition and Subtraction Facts to 12**

13.1 Count On to Add **63**

13.2 Doubles and Doubles Plus 1 . . . . . **64**

13.3 Add 3 Numbers **65**

13.4 Problem Solving • Write a Number Sentence **66**

13.5 Count Back to Subtract **67**

13.6 Subtract to Compare **68**

▶ **Chapter 14: Practice Addition and Subtraction**

14.1 Algebra: Related Addition and Subtraction Facts **69**

14.2 Fact Families to 12 . . . . **70**

14.3 Sums and Differences to 12 . . . . . . **71**

14.4 Algebra: Missing Numbers **72**

14.5 Problem Solving • Choose a Strategy **73**

▶ **Unit 4: GEOMETRY AND ADDITION AND SUBTRACTION TO 20**

▶ **Chapter 15: Solid Figures and Plane Shapes**

15.1 Solid Figures **74**

15.2 Faces and Vertices **75**

15.3 Plane Shapes on Solid Figures **76**

15.4 Sort and Identify Plane Shapes . . . **77**

15.5 Problem Solving • Make a Model . **78**

▶ **Chapter 16: Spatial Sense**

16.1 Open and Closed **79**

16.2 Problem Solving • Use a Picture . . **80**

16.3 Give and Follow Directions **81**

16.4 Symmetry **82**

16.5 Slides and Turns **83**

▶ Chapter 17: Patterns

17.1 Algebra: Describe and Extend
   Patterns **84**

17.2 Algebra: Pattern Units **85**

17.3 Algebra: Make New Patterns **86**

17.4 Problem Solving • Correct
   a Pattern **87**

17.5 Problem Solving • Transfer
   Patterns **88**

▶ Chapter 18: Addition Facts and Strategies

18.1 Doubles and Doubles Plus 1 . . . . . **89**

18.2 10 and More **90**

18.3 Make 10 to Add **91**

18.4 Use Make a 10 . . . . **92**

18.5 Algebra: Add 3 Numbers **93**

18.6 Problem Solving • Use Data
   from a Table **94**

▶ Chapter 19: Subtraction Facts and Strategies

19.1 Use a Number Line to
   Count Back **95**

19.2 Doubles Fact Families **96**

19.3 Algebra: Related Addition and
   Subtraction Facts **97**

19.4 Problem Solving • Estimate
   Reasonable Answers **98**

▶ Chapter 20: Addition and Subtraction Practice

20.1 Practice the Facts **99**

20.2 Fact Families to 20 . . . . **100**

20.3 Algebra: Ways to Make
   Numbers to 20 . . . . **101**

20.4 Problem Solving • Make a
   Model **102**

▶ Unit 5: MONEY, TIME, AND FRACTIONS

▶ Chapter 21: Fractions

21.1 Halves. **103**

21.2 Fourths **104**

21.3 Thirds **105**

21.4 Problem Solving • Use Logical
   Reasoning **106**

21.5 Parts of Groups **107**

▶ Chapter 22: Counting Pennies, Nickels, and Dimes

22.1 Pennies and Nickels **108**

22.2 Pennies and Dimes **109**

22.3 Count Groups of Coins **110**

22.4 Count Collections **111**

22.5 Problem Solving • Make a List . . . **112**

▶ Chapter 23: Using Money

23.1 Trade Pennies, Nickels, and
   Dimes **113**

23.2 Quarters **114**

23.3 Half Dollar and Dollar **115**

23.4 Compare Values **116**

23.5 Same Amounts **117**

23.6 Problem Solving • Act It Out . . . **118**

▶ Chapter 24: Telling Time

24.1 Read a Clock **119**

24.2 Problem Solving • Use
   Estimation **120**

24.3 Time to the Hour **121**

24.4 Tell Time to the Half Hour **122**

24.5 Practice Time to the Hour and
   Half Hour **123**

▶ **Chapter 25: Time and Calendar**
25.1 Use a Calendar **124**
25.2 Daily Events. **125**
25.3 Problem Solving • Make a
     Graph **126**
25.4 Read a Schedule **127**
25.5 Problem Solving • Make
     Reasonable Estimates **128**

▶ **Unit 6: MEASUREMENT, OPERATIONS, AND DATA**

▶ **Chapter 26: Length**
26.1 Compare Lengths **129**
26.2 Use Nonstandard Units **130**
26.3 Inches **131**
26.4 Inches and Feet **132**
26.5 Centimeters **133**
26.6 Problem Solving • Make
     Reasonable Estimates **134**

▶ **Chapter 27: Weight**
27.1 Use a Balance **135**
27.2 Pounds **136**
27.3 Kilograms **137**
27.4 Problem Solving • Predict
     and Test **138**

▶ **Chapter 28: Capacity**
28.1 Nonstandard Units **139**
28.2 Cups, Pints, Quarts **140**
28.3 Liters **141**
28.4 Temperature **142**
28.5 Problem Solving • Choose the
     Measuring Tool **143**

▶ **Chapter 29: Adding and Subtracting 2-Digit Numbers**
29.1 Use Mental Math to Add Tens . . **144**
29.2 Add Tens and Ones **145**
29.3 Add Money **146**
29.4 Use Mental Math to
     Subtract Tens **147**
29.5 Subtract Tens and Ones **148**
29.6 Subtract Money **149**
29.7 Problem Solving • Make
     Reasonable Estimates **150**

▶ **Chapter 30: Probability**
30.1 Certain or Impossible **151**
30.2 More Likely, Less Likely **152**
30.3 Equally Likely **153**
30.4 Problem Solving • Make a
     Prediction **154**

Model Addition Stories

Use ● to tell a story. Draw the ●.
Count. Write how many there are in all.

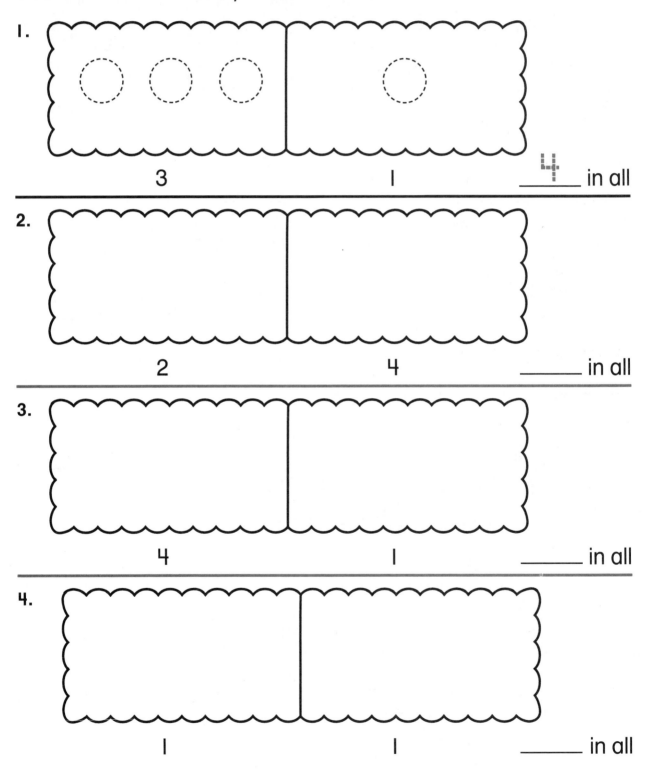

1.

| 3 | 1 | 4 in all |

2.

| 2 | 4 | _____ in all |

3.

| 4 | 1 | _____ in all |

4.

| 1 | 1 | _____ in all |

Use Symbols to Add

Put a ● on each bird.
Add. Write the sum.

1.

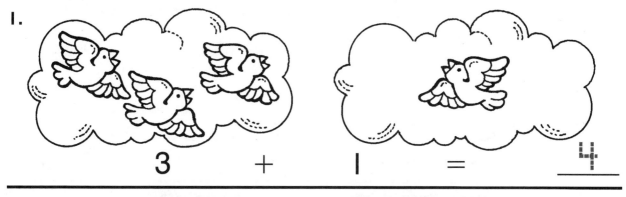

3   +   1   =   4

2.

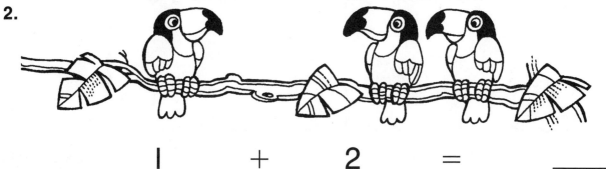

1   +   2   =   ___

3.

2   +   3   =   ___

4.

1   +   1   =   ___

Algebra: Add 0

Use ●. Write the numbers.
Write the sum.

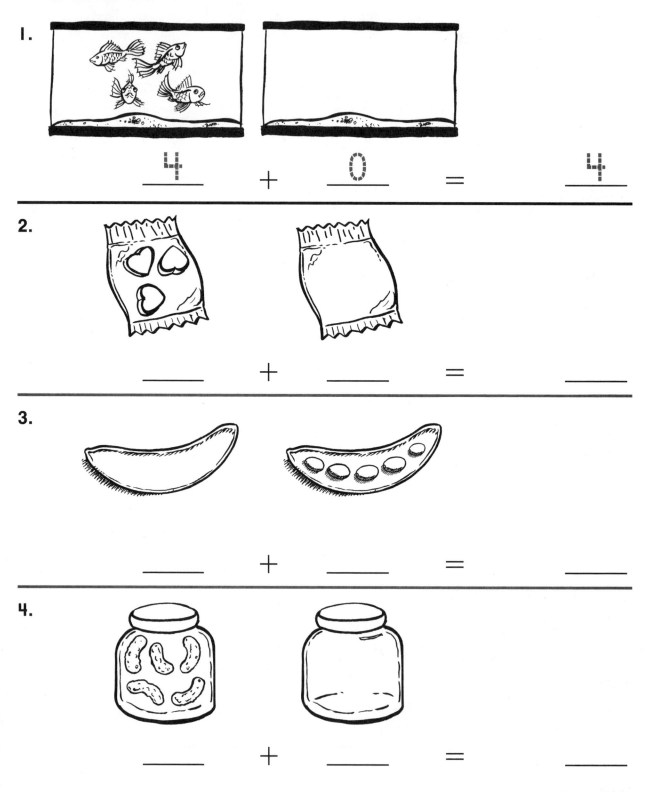

1.   4 + 0 = 4

2.   ___ + ___ = ___

3.   ___ + ___ = ___

4.   ___ + ___ = ___

Problem Solving • Write a Number Sentence

Use ● to show the story.
Then write an addition sentence.

1. 2 brown birds eat.
   1 red bird joins them.
   How many birds are there in all?

   __2__ ⊕ __1__ ⊜ __3__

2. Meg has 3 red balloons.
   She gets 1 blue balloon more.
   How many balloons does she
   have in all?

   ____ ◯ ____ ◯ ____

3. 1 black dog sleeps.
   5 white dogs join him.
   How many dogs are there in all?

   ____ ◯ ____ ◯ ____

4. Sam has 2 red hats.
   He gets 2 green hats more.
   How many hats does he
   have in all?

   ____ ◯ ____ ◯ ____

Algebra: Add in Any Order

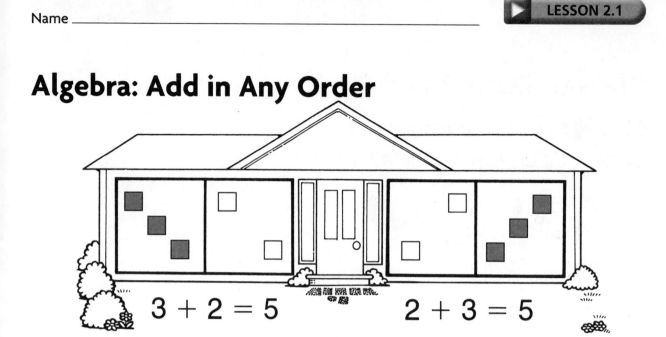

$3 + 2 = 5$ $2 + 3 = 5$

Use 🎲 and 🎲 to find a sum.

Then add in a different order.

Draw 🎲 and 🎲 to show what you do.

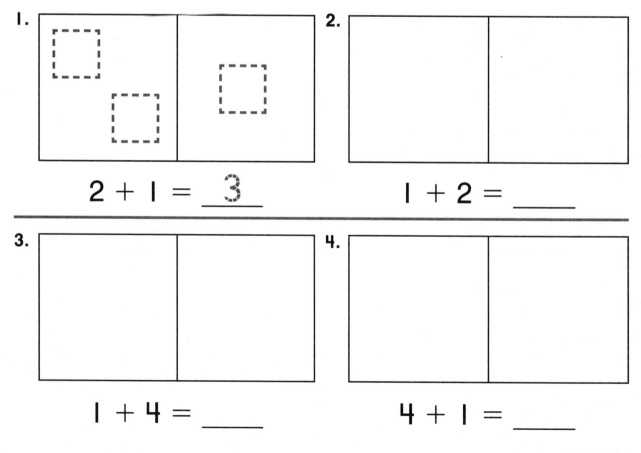

1. $2 + 1 = \underline{\ 3\ }$

2. $1 + 2 = \underline{\ \ \ \ }$

3. $1 + 4 = \underline{\ \ \ \ }$

4. $4 + 1 = \underline{\ \ \ \ }$

Ways to Make 7 and 8

Draw ● to show the numbers.
Color the parts. Write the sum.

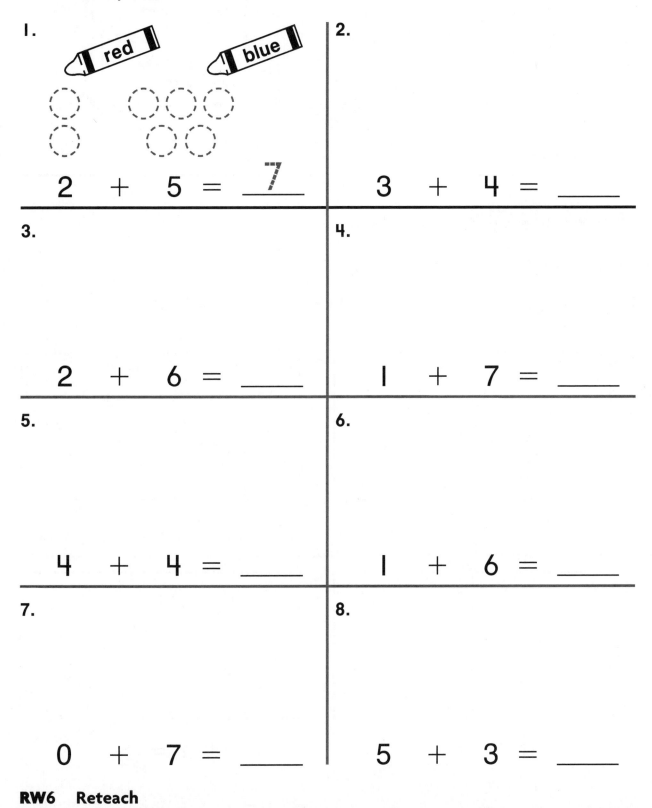

1.

red   blue

2 + 5 = __7__

2.

3 + 4 = ____

3.

2 + 6 = ____

4.

1 + 7 = ____

5.

4 + 4 = ____

6.

1 + 6 = ____

7.

0 + 7 = ____

8.

5 + 3 = ____

Ways to Make 9 and 10

Color each square. Write the numbers.

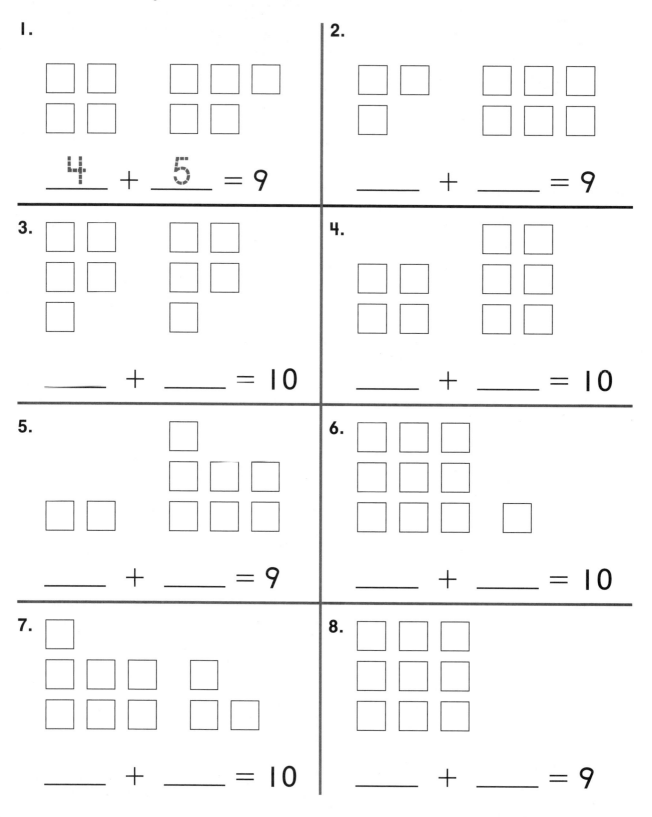

1.

$\underline{4} + \underline{5} = 9$

2.

$\underline{} + \underline{} = 9$

3.

$\underline{} + \underline{} = 10$

4.

$\underline{} + \underline{} = 10$

5.

$\underline{} + \underline{} = 9$

6.

$\underline{} + \underline{} = 10$

7.

$\underline{} + \underline{} = 10$

8.

$\underline{} + \underline{} = 9$

Vertical Addition

$2 + 1 = 3$

$$\begin{array}{r} 2 \\ + 1 \\ \hline 3 \end{array}$$

Use ● to add. Draw them.
Write the sum.

1. ○   ○ ○ ○

$1 + 3 = \underline{4}$

2.
$$\begin{array}{r} 1 \\ + 3 \\ \hline 4 \end{array}$$
○   ○ ○ ○

3.

$3 + 2 = \underline{}$

4.
$$\begin{array}{r} 3 \\ + 2 \\ \hline \end{array}$$

5.

$1 + 5 = \underline{}$

6.
$$\begin{array}{r} 1 \\ + 5 \\ \hline \end{array}$$

7.

$2 + 2 = \underline{}$

8
$$\begin{array}{r} 2 \\ + 2 \\ \hline \end{array}$$

Problem Solving • Make a Model

Put a ⬤ on each circle to show the price.
Draw the (1¢). Add. Write how much you spend.

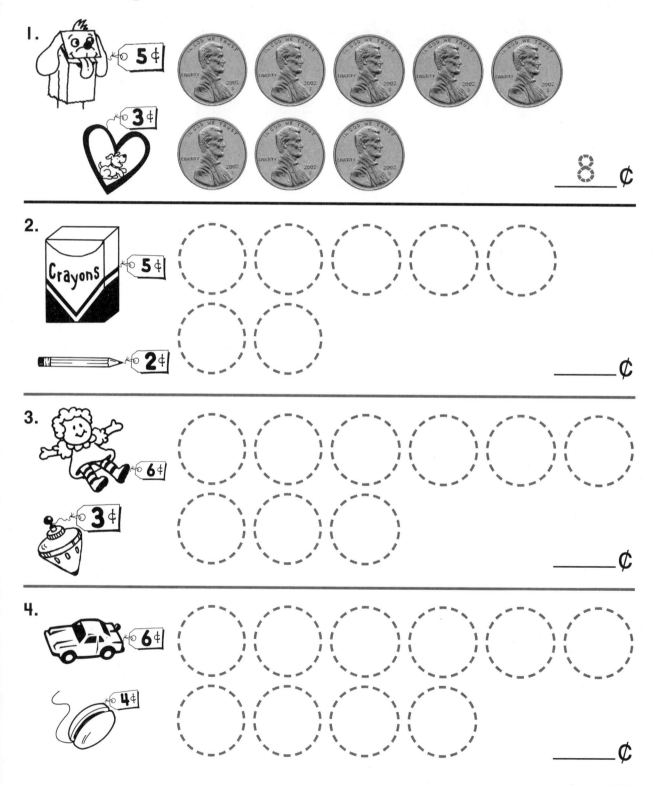

1.
5¢
3¢
8 ¢

2.
Crayons
5¢
2¢
_____ ¢

3.
6¢
3¢
_____ ¢

4.
6¢
4¢
_____ ¢

Model Subtraction Stories

Tell a story about the picture.
Use ● to show it. Write how many are left.

1.

3 raccoons   **2** go away.   _____ is left.

2.

4 birds   **1** goes away.   _____ are left.

3.

5 rabbits   **3** go away.   _____ are left.

4.

2 beavers   **1** goes away.   _____ is left.

Use Symbols to Subtract

Use ●.
Write the difference.

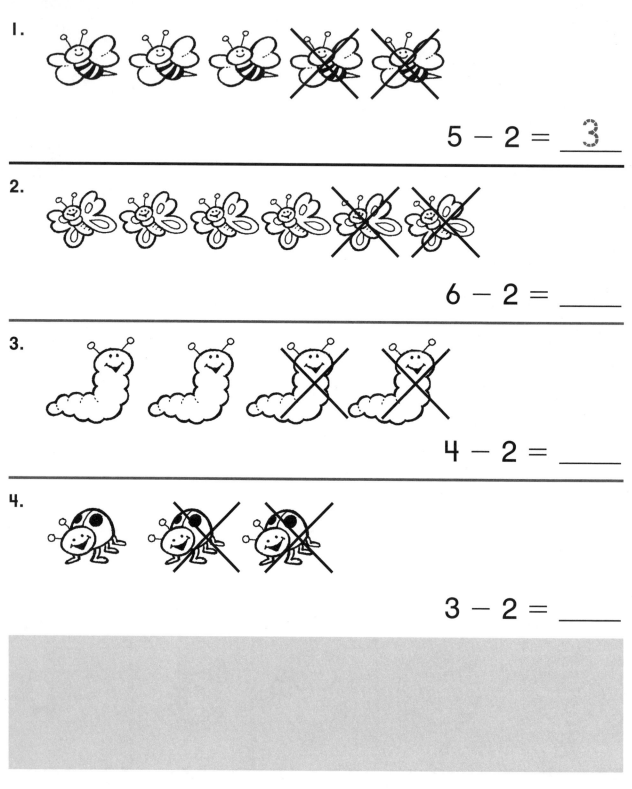

1.

$$5 - 2 = \underline{3}$$

2.

$$6 - 2 = \underline{}$$

3.

$$4 - 2 = \underline{}$$

4.

$$3 - 2 = \underline{}$$

Algebra: Write Subtraction Sentences

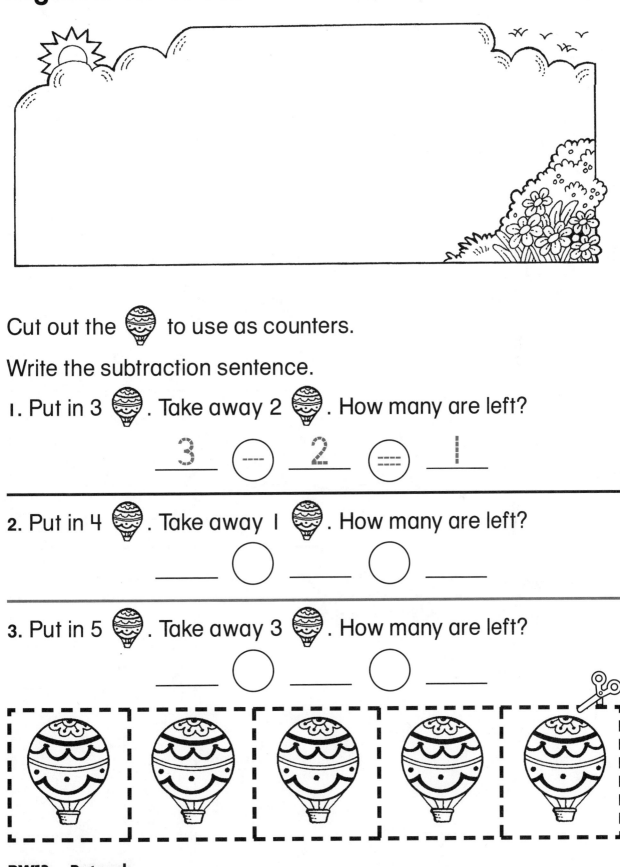

Cut out the 🎈 to use as counters.

Write the subtraction sentence.

1. Put in 3 🎈. Take away 2 🎈. How many are left?

    _3_ (_-_) _2_ (_=_) _1_

2. Put in 4 🎈. Take away 1 🎈. How many are left?

    ___ ( ) ___ ( ) ___

3. Put in 5 🎈. Take away 3 🎈. How many are left?

    ___ ( ) ___ ( ) ___

Problem Solving • Make a Model

Draw a line to match the story with the model.
Write the difference.

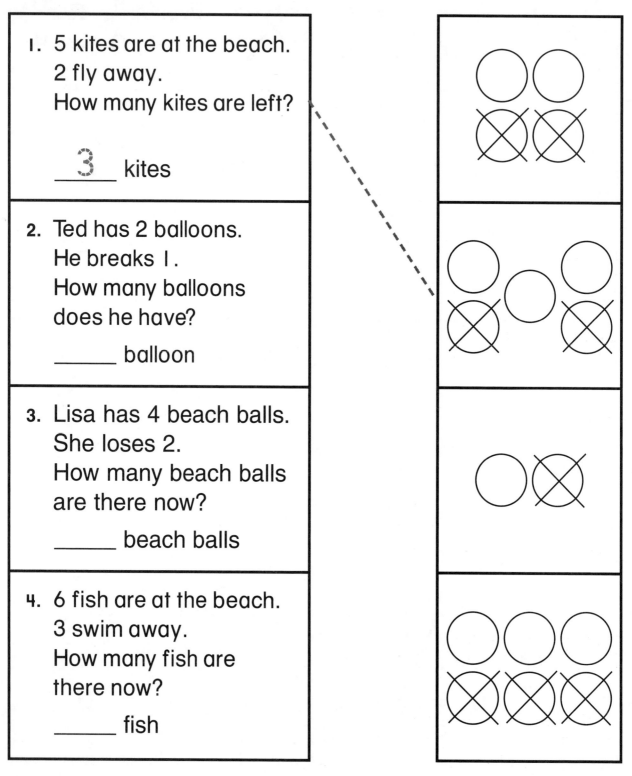

1. 5 kites are at the beach.
   2 fly away.
   How many kites are left?

   __3__ kites

2. Ted has 2 balloons.
   He breaks 1.
   How many balloons
   does he have?

   _____ balloon

3. Lisa has 4 beach balls.
   She loses 2.
   How many beach balls
   are there now?

   _____ beach balls

4. 6 fish are at the beach.
   3 swim away.
   How many fish are
   there now?

   _____ fish

Algebra: Subtract All or Zero

Circle the number sentence that matches the picture.

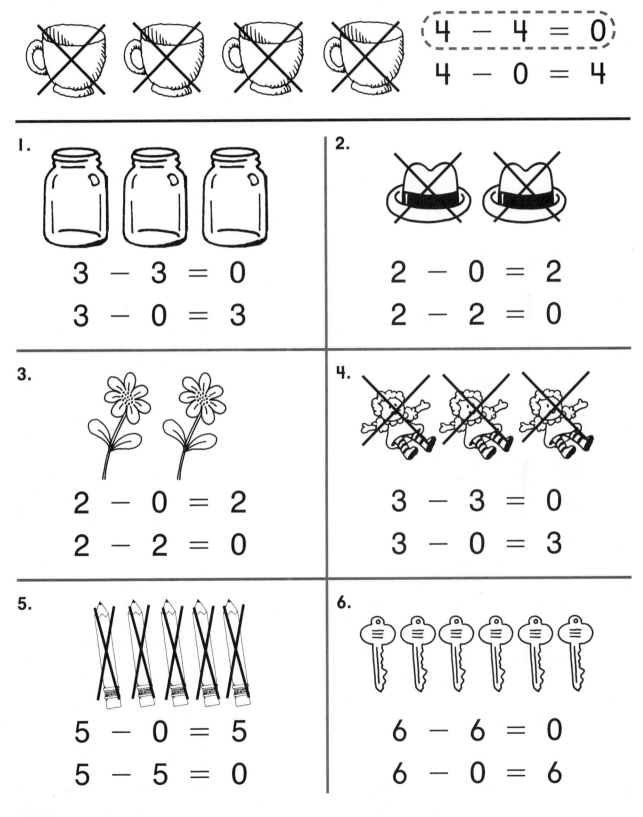

4 – 4 = 0

4 – 0 = 4

1.

3 – 3 = 0

3 – 0 = 3

2.

2 – 0 = 2

2 – 2 = 0

3.

2 – 0 = 2

2 – 2 = 0

4.

3 – 3 = 0

3 – 0 = 3

5.

5 – 0 = 5

5 – 5 = 0

6.

6 – 6 = 0

6 – 0 = 6

Take Apart 7 and 8

Use the picture.
Circle the number sentence that matches.
Write the difference.

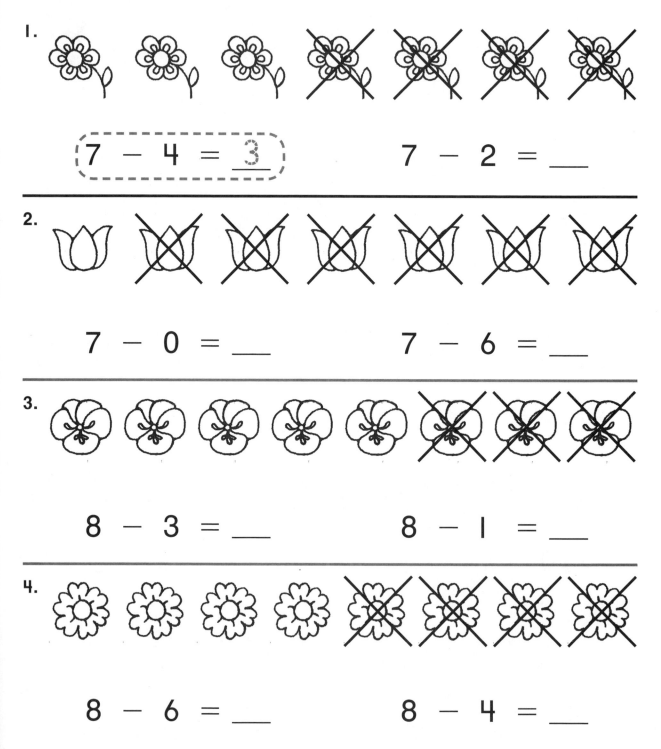

1.

$7 - 4 = \underline{3}$ $7 - 2 = \underline{}$

2.

$7 - 0 = \underline{}$ $7 - 6 = \underline{}$

3.

$8 - 3 = \underline{}$ $8 - 1 = \underline{}$

4.

$8 - 6 = \underline{}$ $8 - 4 = \underline{}$

Take Apart 9 and 10

Use ●.
Circle the number sentence that matches the picture.
Write the difference.

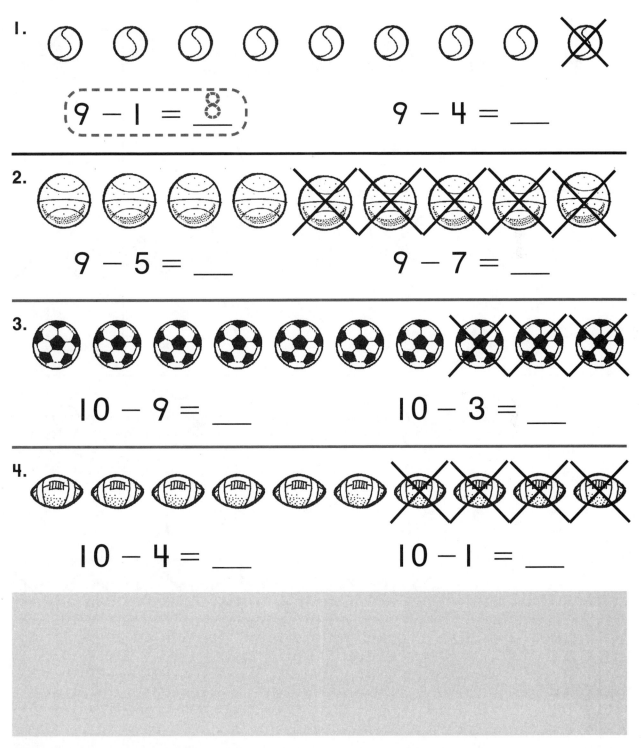

1.

$9 - 1 = \underline{8}$ $9 - 4 = \underline{}$

2.

$9 - 5 = \underline{}$ $9 - 7 = \underline{}$

3.

$10 - 9 = \underline{}$ $10 - 3 = \underline{}$

4.

$10 - 4 = \underline{}$ $10 - 1 = \underline{}$

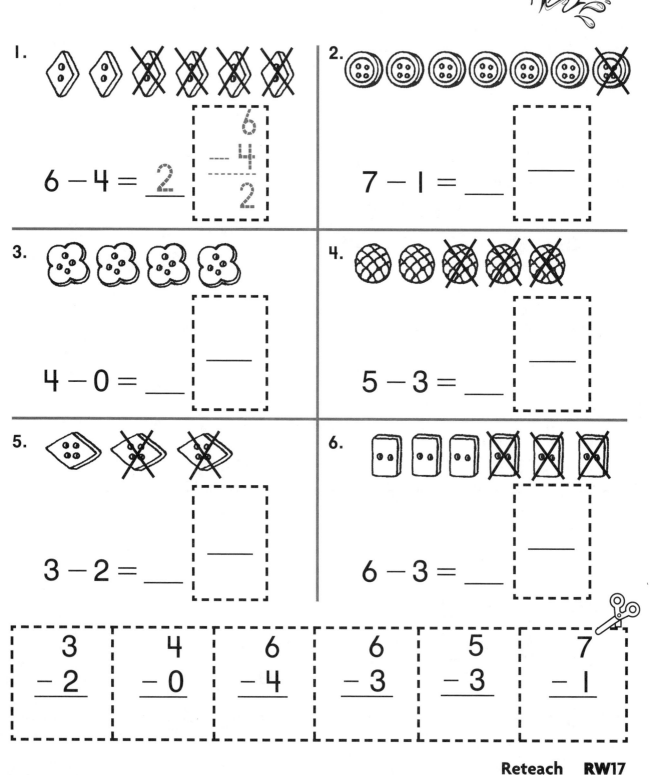

Vertical Subtraction

Match the subtraction problems.
Cut and paste.
Solve.

1. $6 - 4 = \underline{2}$

$$\begin{array}{r} 6 \\ -\ 4 \\ \hline 2 \end{array}$$

2. $7 - 1 = \underline{}$

3. $4 - 0 = \underline{}$

4. $5 - 3 = \underline{}$

5. $3 - 2 = \underline{}$

6. $6 - 3 = \underline{}$

$$\begin{array}{r} 3 \\ -\ 2 \\ \hline \end{array} \qquad \begin{array}{r} 4 \\ -\ 0 \\ \hline \end{array} \qquad \begin{array}{r} 6 \\ -\ 4 \\ \hline \end{array} \qquad \begin{array}{r} 6 \\ -\ 3 \\ \hline \end{array} \qquad \begin{array}{r} 5 \\ -\ 3 \\ \hline \end{array} \qquad \begin{array}{r} 7 \\ -\ 1 \\ \hline \end{array}$$

Subtract to Compare

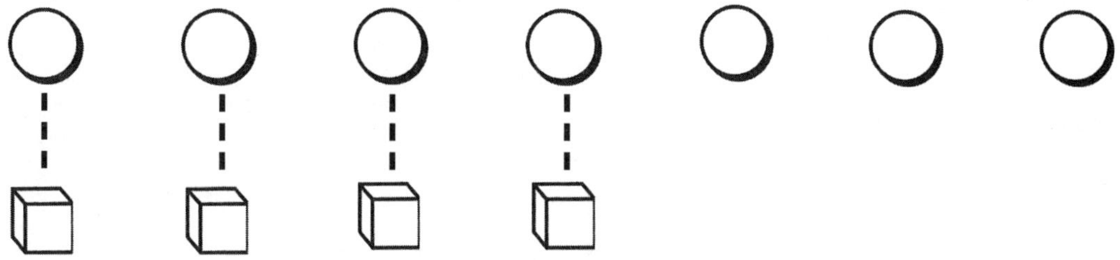

$7 - 4 = \underline{3}$

There are 3 more ○.

Draw lines to match.
Subtract. Circle how many more.

1.

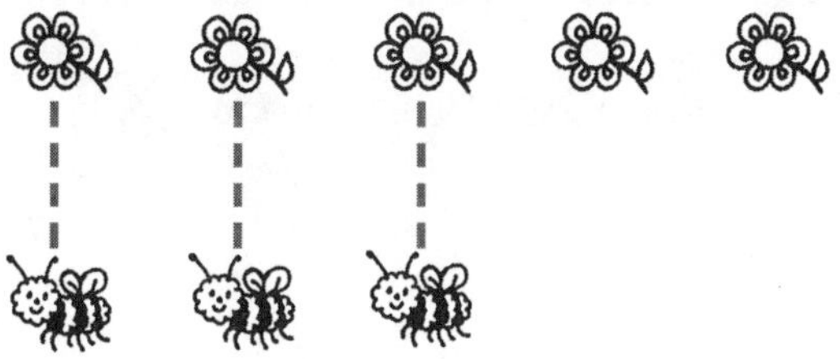

$5 - 3 = \underline{2}$

(2 more 🌸)
3 more 🌸

2.

$6 - 3 = \underline{}$

6 more 🐤
3 more 🐤

3.

$6 - 5 = \underline{}$

1 more 🍃
5 more 🍃

4.

$4 - 2 = \underline{}$

2 more 🐿
4 more 🐿

Name _____

Problem Solving • Draw a Picture

Draw a picture to show the problem.
Write how many were given away.

1. Carl had 4 pencils.
He gave some to his friends.
He has 1 pencil left.
How many pencils did
Carl give to his friends?
___3___ pencils

What number can I add to 1 to make 4?

2. Rachel had 7 paintbrushes.
She gave some to her friends.
She has 3 paintbrushes left.
How many paintbrushes
did Rachel give to her friends?
_____ paintbrushes

What number can I add to 3 to make 7?

3. Cole had 8 markers.
He gave some to his friends.
He has 5 markers left.
How many markers did
Cole give to his friends?
_____ markers

What number can I add to 5 to make 8?

4. Marcy had 5 crayons.
She gave some to her friends.
She has 2 crayons left.
How many crayons did
Marcy give to her friends?
_____ crayons

What number can I add to 2 to make 5?

Count On 1 and 2

Count on. Write the sum.

1.

Say 8. Count on 2.
9, 10

8

$\underset{9}{\rule{1cm}{0.4pt}}$, $\underset{10}{\rule{1cm}{0.4pt}}$

$8 + 2 = \underline{10}$

2.

5

___

$5 + 1 = \underline{}$

3.

3

___ , ___

$3 + 2 = \underline{}$

4.

7

___ , ___

$7 + 2 = \underline{}$

5.

4

___ , ___

$4 + 2 = \underline{}$

6.

6

___

$6 + 1 = \underline{}$

Use a Number Line to Count On

Use the number line to count on.
Write the sum.

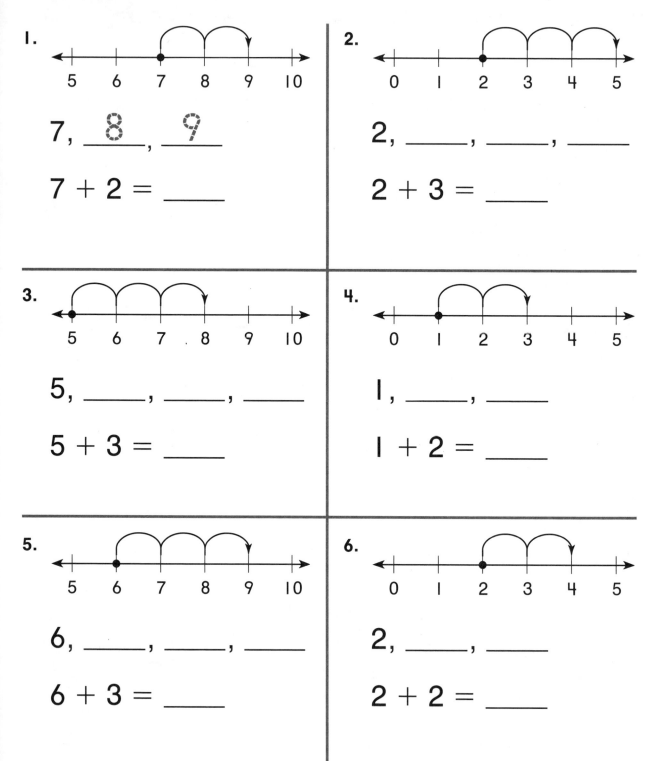

1.

5　6　7　8　9　10

7, _8_, _9_

7 + 2 = ___

2.

0　1　2　3　4　5

2, ___, ___, ___

2 + 3 = ___

3.

5　6　7　8　9　10

5, ___, ___, ___

5 + 3 = ___

4.

0　1　2　3　4　5

1, ___, ___

1 + 2 = ___

5.

5　6　7　8　9　10

6, ___, ___, ___

6 + 3 = ___

6.

0　1　2　3　4　5

2, ___, ___

2 + 2 = ___

Use Doubles

Make a double.
Draw the same number of dots.
Complete the doubles fact.

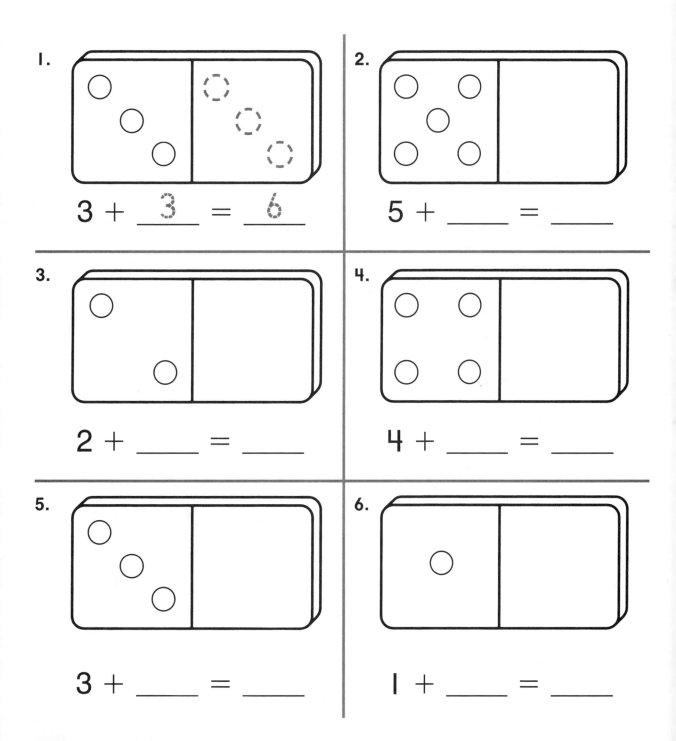

1.

$3 +$ _3_ $=$ _6_

2.

$5 +$ ___ $=$ ___

3.

$2 +$ ___ $=$ ___

4.

$4 +$ ___ $=$ ___

5.

$3 +$ ___ $=$ ___

6.

$1 +$ ___ $=$ ___

Problem Solving • Draw a Picture

Draw a picture to solve.

1. 4 shells are on the beach.
2 shells are in the water.
How many shells are there?

___6___ shells

2. There are 5 whales swimming.
3 more whales join them.
How many whales are there?

_____ whales

3. There are 3 crabs on the sand.
2 more crabs come.
How many crabs are there?

_____ crabs

4. There are 6 large birds.
There are 3 small birds.
How many birds are there?

_____ birds

Use the Strategies

Count on. Write the numbers.
Write the sum.

1. $6 + 1 = \underline{\ ?\ }$
Say 6.
Count on 1.

6, _7_

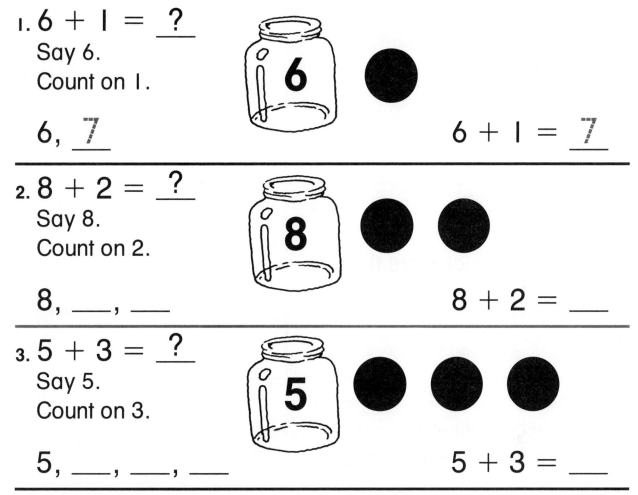

$6 + 1 = \underline{7}$

2. $8 + 2 = \underline{\ ?\ }$
Say 8.
Count on 2.

8, ___, ___

$8 + 2 = \underline{\ \ }$

3. $5 + 3 = \underline{\ ?\ }$
Say 5.
Count on 3.

5, ___, ___, ___

$5 + 3 = \underline{\ \ }$

Look at the number.
Add its double. Write the sum.

4. $3 + \underline{\ \ } = \underline{\ \ }$

5. $5 + \underline{\ \ } = \underline{\ \ }$

Sums to 8

Add. Change the order.
Add again.

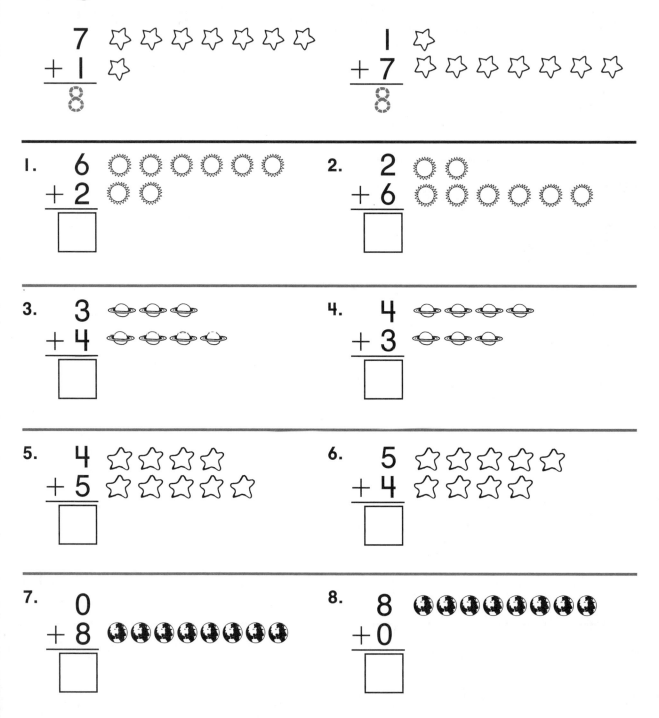

7
+ 1

8

1
+ 7

8

1. 6
   + 2
   ---

2. 2
   + 6
   ---

3. 3
   + 4
   ---

4. 4
   + 3
   ---

5. 4
   + 5
   ---

6. 5
   + 4
   ---

7. 0
   + 8
   ---

8. 8
   + 0

Sums to 10

Add. Use the pictures to help.

1.   9
   + 0
   ⬚ 9

2.   0
   + 9
   ⬚ 9

3.   7
   + 3
   ⬚

4.   3
   + 7
   ⬚

5.   1
   + 6
   ⬚

6.   6
   + 1
   ⬚

7.   6
   + 4
   ⬚

8.   4
   + 6
   ⬚

9.   2
   + 7
   ⬚

10.   7
   + 2
   ⬚

Algebra: Follow the Rule

Add 1	
1	2
3	4
5	6

The rule is add 1.

$$1 + 1 = 2$$
$$3 + 1 = 4$$
$$5 + 1 = 6$$

Complete the table.
Follow the rule.

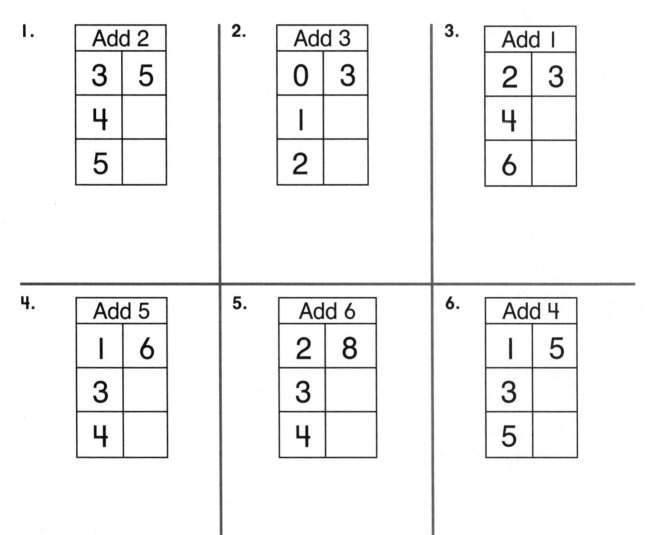

1.

Add 2	
3	5
4	
5	

2.

Add 3	
0	3
1	
2	

3.

Add 1	
2	3
4	
6	

4.

Add 5	
1	6
3	
4	

5.

Add 6	
2	8
3	
4	

6.

Add 4	
1	5
3	
5	

Problem Solving • Write a Number Sentence

Solve. Write a number sentence.
Use ● ○ to check.

1. Dan has 4 crayons.
   He finds 3 more.
   How many crayons
   does he have now?

   ○○○○ crayons
   ●●● crayons

   4 (+) 3 (=) 7

2. Ming draws 5 pictures.
   Alex draws 3 pictures.
   How many pictures
   do they draw in all?

   ____ ◯ ____ ◯ ____ pictures

3. Jana does 6 jumping jacks.
   Then she does 4 more.
   How many jumping jacks
   does she do in all?

   ____ ◯ ____ ◯ ____ jumping jacks

4. 4 boys sit at a lunch table.
   5 girls join them.
   How many children
   are at the lunch table?

   ____ ◯ ____ ◯ ____ children

Use a Number Line to Count Back 1 and 2

Use the number line. **Count back** to subtract.

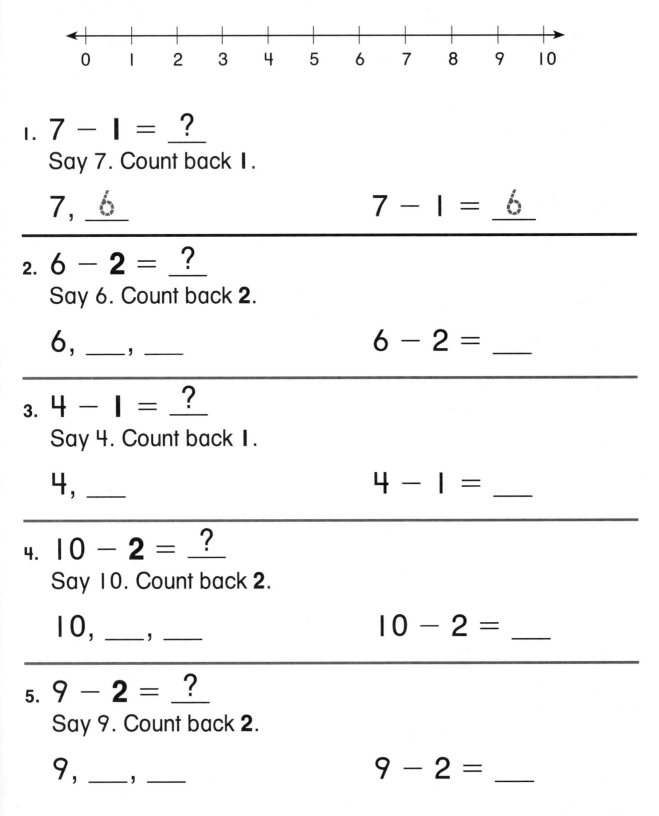

0   1   2   3   4   5   6   7   8   9   10

1. $7 - 1 = \underline{?}$
Say 7. Count back 1.

7, _6_ $7 - 1 = \underline{6}$

2. $6 - 2 = \underline{?}$
Say 6. Count back 2.

6, ___, ___ $6 - 2 = \underline{}$

3. $4 - 1 = \underline{?}$
Say 4. Count back 1.

4, ___ $4 - 1 = \underline{}$

4. $10 - 2 = \underline{?}$
Say 10. Count back 2.

10, ___, ___ $10 - 2 = \underline{}$

5. $9 - 2 = \underline{?}$
Say 9. Count back 2.

9, ___, ___ $9 - 2 = \underline{}$

Use a Number Line to Count Back 3

Use the number line. **Count back** to subtract.

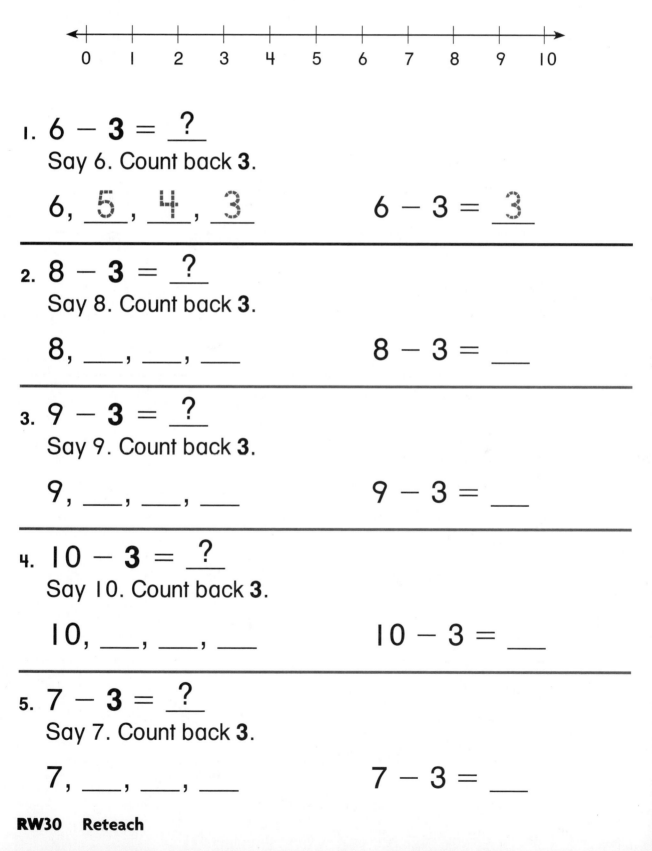

1. $6 - 3 =$ _?_

   Say 6. Count back **3**.

   6, _5_, _4_, _3_ $6 - 3 = $ _3_

2. $8 - 3 =$ _?_

   Say 8. Count back **3**.

   8, ___, ___, ___ $8 - 3 = $ ___

3. $9 - 3 =$ _?_

   Say 9. Count back **3**.

   9, ___, ___, ___ $9 - 3 = $ ___

4. $10 - 3 =$ _?_

   Say 10. Count back **3**.

   10, ___, ___, ___ $10 - 3 = $ ___

5. $7 - 3 =$ _?_

   Say 7. Count back **3**.

   7, ___, ___, ___ $7 - 3 = $ ___

Algebra: Relate Addition and Subtraction

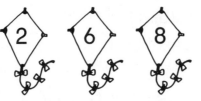

2 + 6 = 8 has the same numbers as 8 − 6 = 2.
They are related facts.

___

Use 🎲.

Complete the subtraction sentence.

Addition Sentence	Subtraction Sentence
1. $5 + 2 = 7$	$\boxed{7} - \boxed{2} = 5$
2. $6 + 1 = 7$	$\boxed{} - \boxed{} = 6$
3. $1 + 3 = 4$	$\boxed{} - \boxed{} = 1$
4. $2 + 4 = 6$	$\boxed{} - \boxed{} = 2$
5. $4 + 4 = 8$	$\boxed{} - \boxed{} = 4$
6. $3 + 0 = 3$	$\boxed{} - \boxed{} = 3$

Name _____

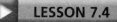

Problem Solving • Draw a Picture

Subtract. Cross out pictures.
Use counters if you need them.

1. There are 5 butterflies on a flower.
   Then 2 fly away.
   How many butterflies are still
   on the flower?

   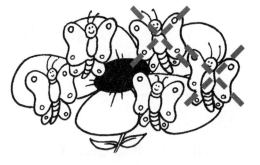

   ___3___ butterflies

---

2. There are 6 balloons in the air.
   Then 4 land on the ground.
   How many balloons are
   in the air now?

   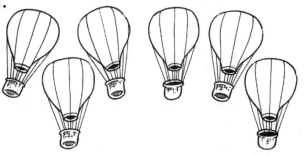

   _____ balloons

---

3. There are 7 children flying kites.
   Then 4 children go home.
   How many children are still
   flying kites?

   _____ children

---

4. There are 10 birds in a tree.
   Then 6 fly away.
   How many birds are still
   in the tree?

   _____ birds

Use the Strategies

Cross out pictures to subtract.
Write the difference.

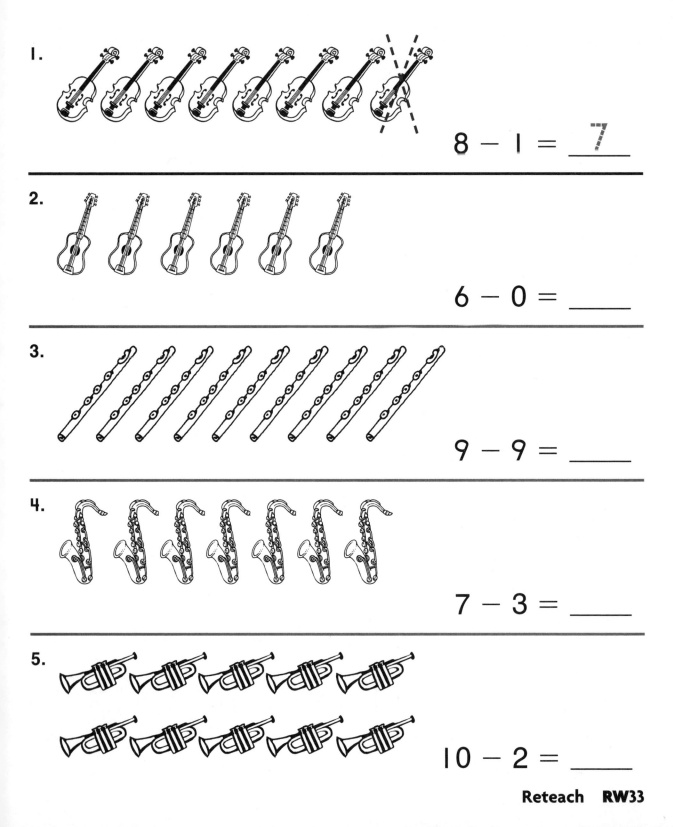

1. $8 - 1 = \underline{7}$

2. $6 - 0 = \underline{}$

3. $9 - 9 = \underline{}$

4. $7 - 3 = \underline{}$

5. $10 - 2 = \underline{}$

Subtraction to 10

Match the picture to the subtraction sentence.

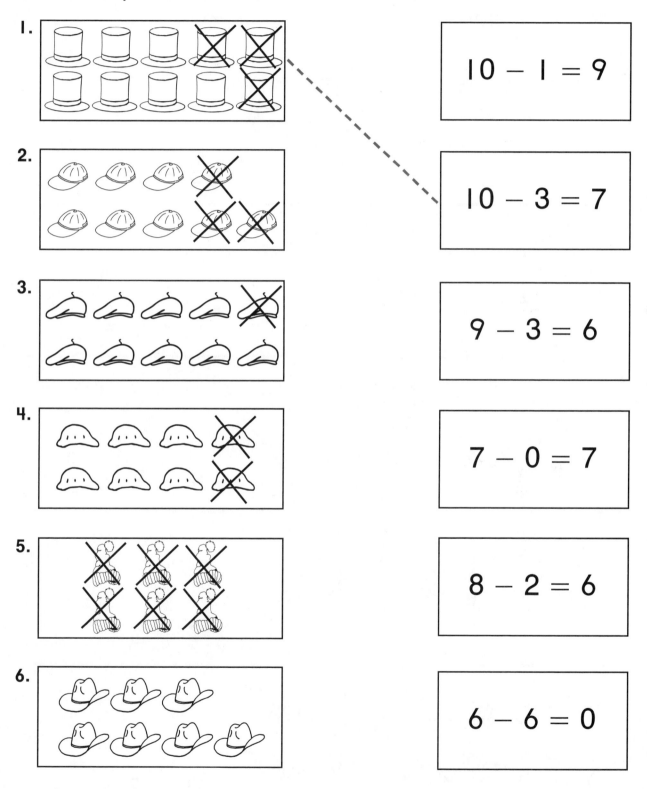

1.

2.

3.

4.

5.

6.

$$10 - 1 = 9$$

$$10 - 3 = 7$$

$$9 - 3 = 6$$

$$7 - 0 = 7$$

$$8 - 2 = 6$$

$$6 - 6 = 0$$

Algebra: Follow the Rule

Follow the rule. Solve.
Cross out pictures to help.

1.

Subtract 2		
3	$-$ __2__ $=$	__1__
4	$-$ ____ $=$	____
5	$-$ ____ $=$	____

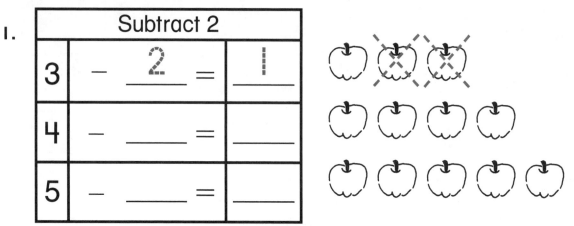

2.

Subtract 1		
3	$-$ ____ $=$	____
4	$-$ ____ $=$	____
5	$-$ ____ $=$	____

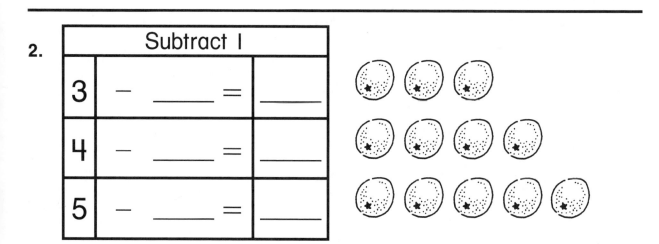

3.

Subtract 3		
3	$-$ ____ $=$	____
4	$-$ ____ $=$	____
5	$-$ ____ $=$	____

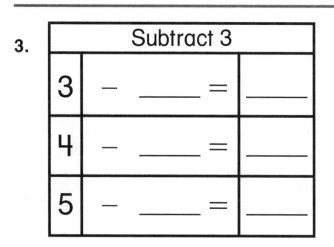

Fact Families to 10

2, 3, and 5 are the numbers in this **fact family**.

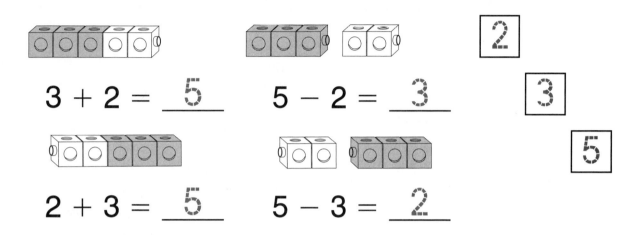

$3 + 2 = \underline{5}$ $5 - 2 = \underline{3}$ $\boxed{2}$

$\boxed{3}$

$\boxed{5}$

$2 + 3 = \underline{5}$ $5 - 3 = \underline{2}$

Add or subtract.

Write the numbers in each fact family.

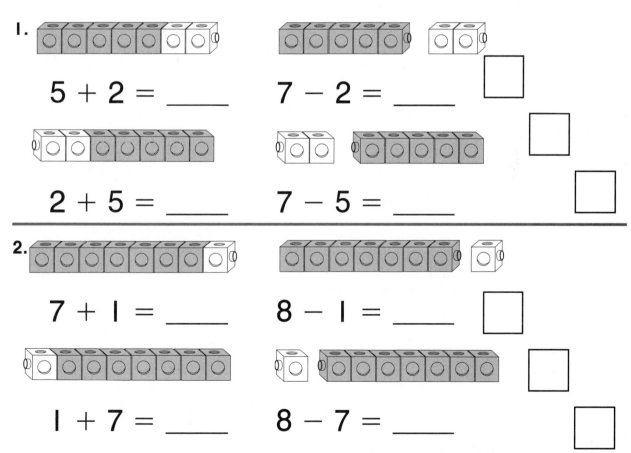

1.

$5 + 2 = \underline{}$ $7 - 2 = \underline{}$

$\boxed{}$

$\boxed{}$

$2 + 5 = \underline{}$ $7 - 5 = \underline{}$

$\boxed{}$

2.

$7 + 1 = \underline{}$ $8 - 1 = \underline{}$

$\boxed{}$

$\boxed{}$

$1 + 7 = \underline{}$ $8 - 7 = \underline{}$

$\boxed{}$

Name _____

Problem Solving • Choose the Operation

You can add or subtract to solve problems.
Circle the number sentence to show what you do.
Write the answer.

1. Ruth has 5 apples.
   She gives 2 away.
   How many apples
   does Ruth have now?

   $5 + 2 = 7$

   $(5 - 2 = 3)$

   __3__ apples

2. Lee's mom has 6 carrots.
   She uses 4 to make soup.
   How many carrots does
   she have now?

   $6 + 4 = 10$

   $6 - 4 = 2$

   _____ carrots

3. Tina picks 8 peaches.
   She gives 3 to her friends.
   How many peaches does
   Tina have now?

   $8 + 3 = 11$

   $8 - 3 = 5$

   _____ peaches

4. Sam has 4 sandwiches.
   He makes 3 more.
   How many sandwiches does
   Sam have now?

   $4 + 3 = 7$

   $4 - 3 = 1$

   _____ sandwiches

Algebra: Sort and Classify

Circle each cat that belongs in Group A.

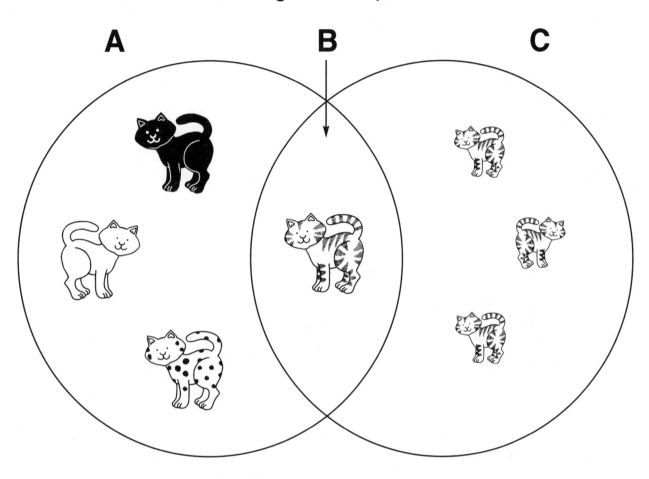

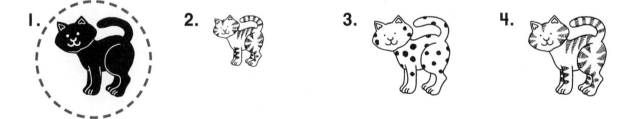

1.   2.   3.   4.

Make Concrete Graphs

Sort the shapes. Use Attribute Links if you need to.
Draw the shapes in the graph.
Cross off each shape as you draw it.

Kinds of Shapes

△	△				
○					
☐					

Use the graph to answer the questions.

1. How many ☐ are there? _____

2. How many ○ are there? _____

3. How many more △ than ☐ are there? _____

4. How many shapes in all are △ and ○? _____

Make Picture Graphs

Vegetables We Like					
carrots	🥕	🥕	🥕	🥕	
peas	🌿	🌿			
potatoes	🥔	🥔	🥔	🥔	🥔
broccoli	🥦				

Use the graph. Circle how many there are.

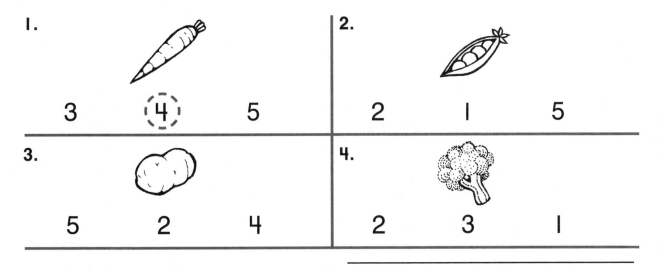

1. 🥕   3   (4)   5

2. 🫛   2   1   5

3. 🥔   5   2   4

4. 🥦   2   3   1

5. Which vegetable did
   the most children choose?   _____

Read a Tally Table

1. Color each large circle | blue |▷ .
   Color each small circle | red |▷ .

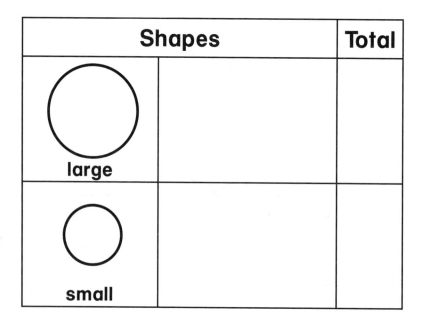

2. Fill in the tally table to show each large circle
   and each small circle.

Shapes		Total
large		
small		

Make Bar Graphs

Some children talked about the ways they go to school.
Then they made a graph.

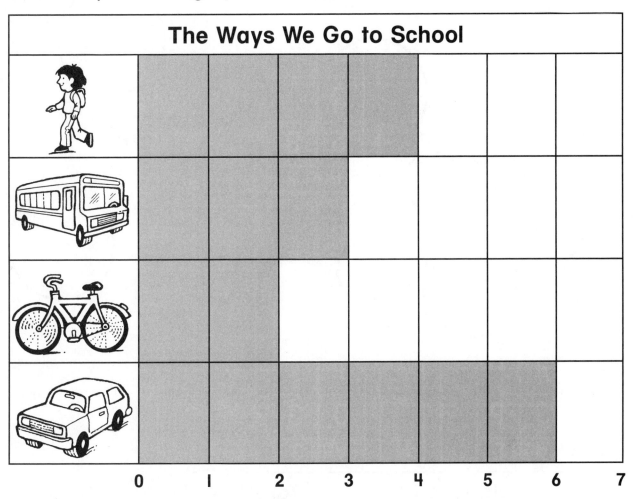

How many children go to school each way?
Write how many.

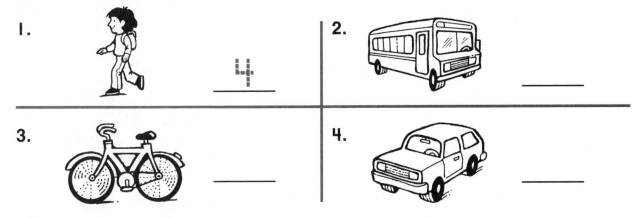

1.   2.

    4   _____

3.   4.

    _____   _____

Name _____

Problem Solving • Use Data from a Graph

Use the bar graph to answer the questions.
Use ⬚ if you need help.

Our Favorite Pets

	0	1	2	3	4	5	6
Dogs							
Cats							
Birds							

1. How many children chose 🐕 or 🐈?

   _____ children

   Think: You can add to solve a problem.

   5 ⊕ 4 ⊜ 9

2. How many more children chose 🐈 than 🐦?

   _____ child

   Think: You can subtract to solve a problem.

   ___ ◯ ___ ◯ ___

3. Did more children choose 🐕 or 🐦?

   _____

   How many more children made that choice?

   _____ children

   Think: How many chose each pet?

   _____ children chose 🐕.

   _____ children chose 🐦.

   Think: I can subtract.

   ___ ◯ ___ ◯ ___

Interpret Graphs

Use the graph to answer the questions.

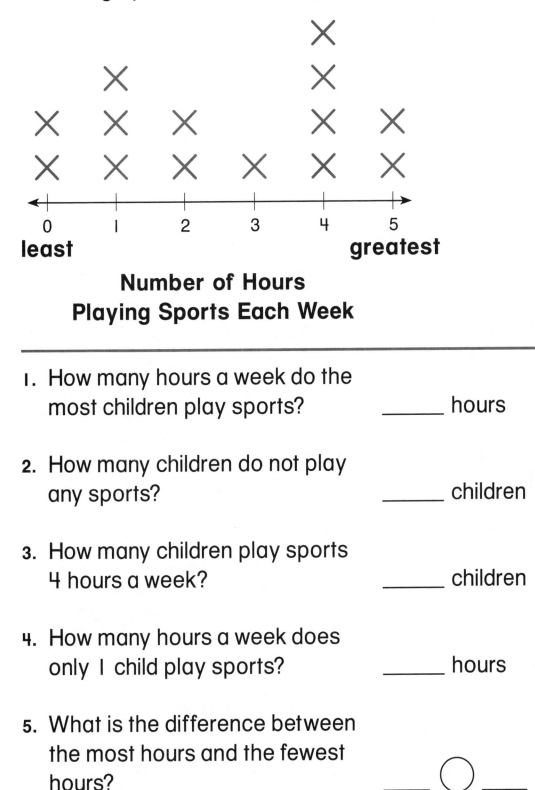

least   greatest

**Number of Hours
Playing Sports Each Week**

---

1. How many hours a week do the most children play sports? _____ hours

2. How many children do not play any sports? _____ children

3. How many children play sports 4 hours a week? _____ children

4. How many hours a week does only 1 child play sports? _____ hours

5. What is the difference between the most hours and the fewest hours? ___ ◯ ___ ◯ ___

Teen Numbers

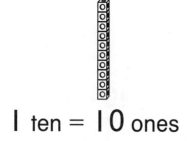

I ten = 10 ones   I one = I

Use 🔲 to show the tens and ones.
Write the number.

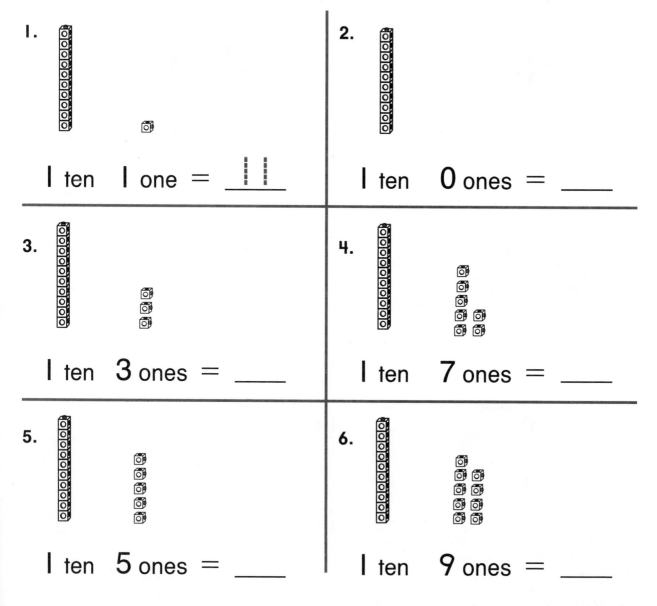

1.

I ten   I one = __I I__

2.

I ten   0 ones = ____

3.

I ten   3 ones = ____

4.

I ten   7 ones = ____

5.

I ten   5 ones = ____

6.

I ten   9 ones = ____

Tens

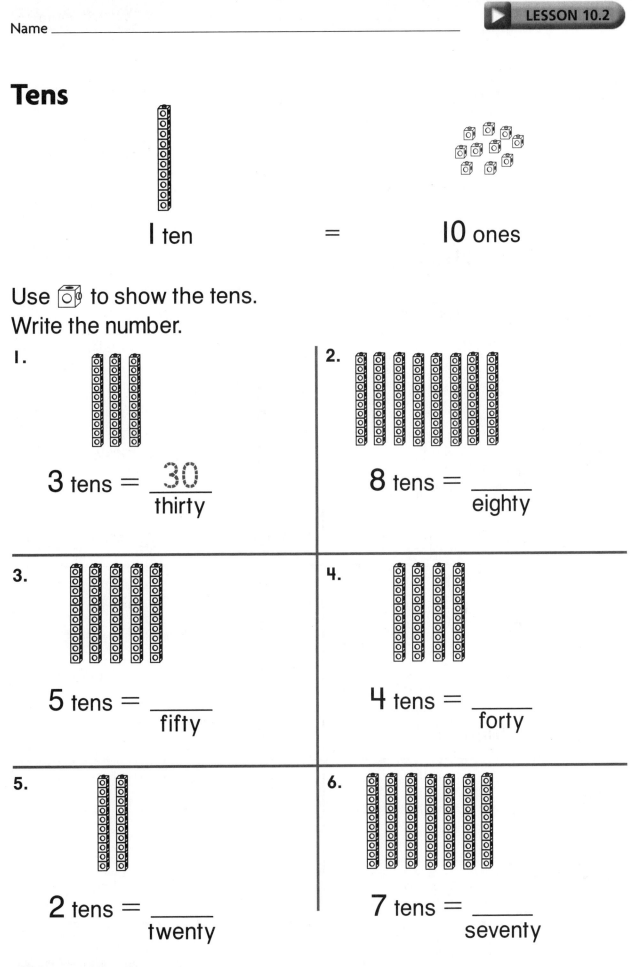

I ten   =   10 ones

Use 🔲 to show the tens.
Write the number.

1.

3 tens = __30__
         thirty

2.

8 tens = _____
         eighty

3.

5 tens = _____
         fifty

4.

4 tens = _____
         forty

5.

2 tens = _____
         twenty

6.

7 tens = _____
         seventy

Tens and Ones to 50

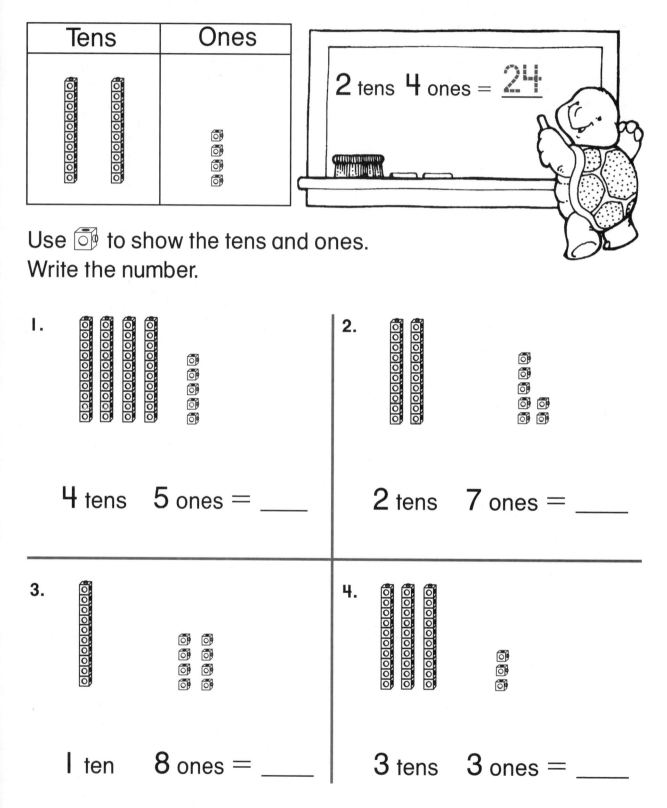

Tens	Ones

2 tens 4 ones = 24

Use 🔲 to show the tens and ones.
Write the number.

1. 4 tens 5 ones = ____

2. 2 tens 7 ones = ____

3. 1 ten 8 ones = ____

4. 3 tens 3 ones = ____

Tens and Ones to 100

Tens	Ones

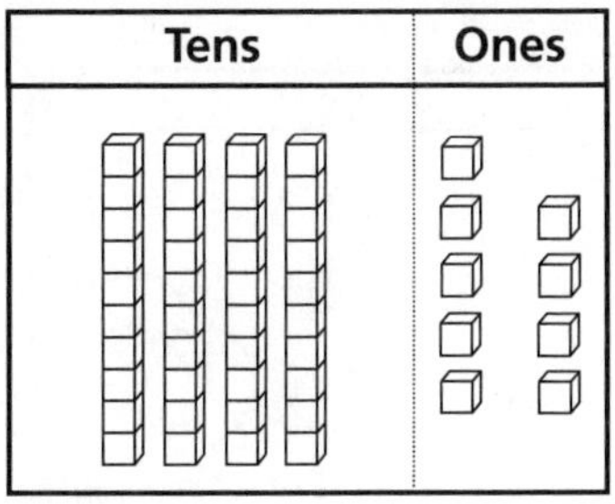

4 tens 9 ones = 49

Use ▱ and ▭▭▭▭ .
Write the number.

1.

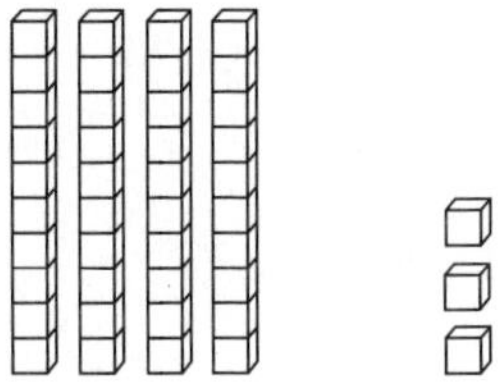

4 tens   3 ones = ____

2.

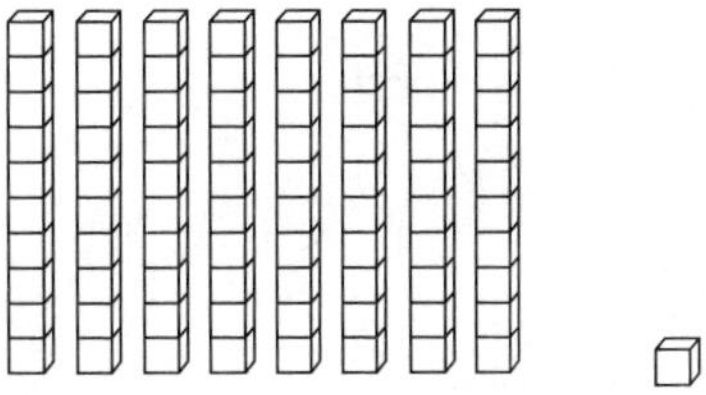

8 tens   1 one = ____

3.

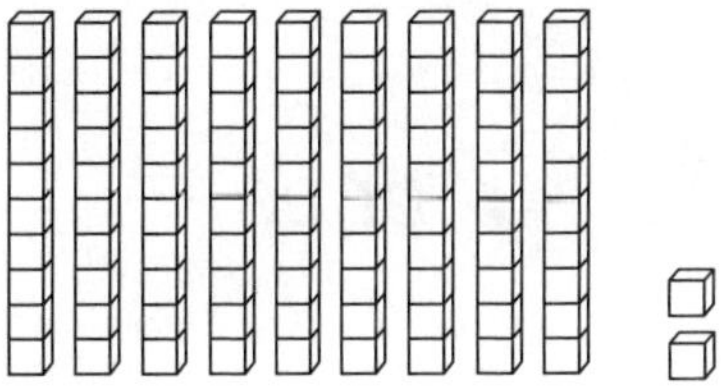

9 tens   2 ones = ____

4.

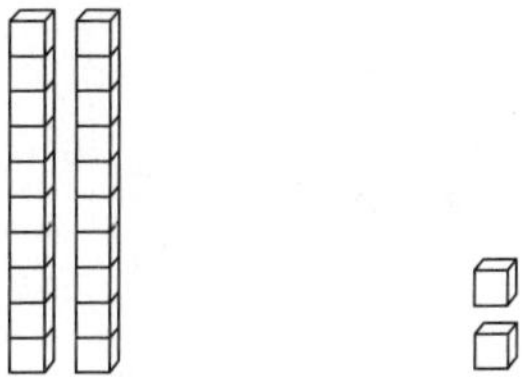

2 tens   2 ones = ____

5.

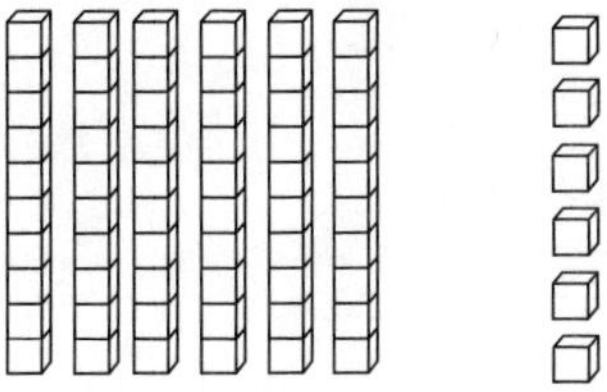

6 tens   6 ones = ____

6.

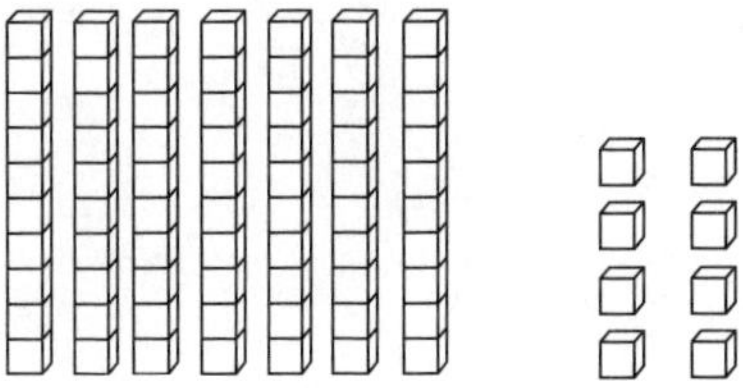

7 tens   8 ones = ____

Algebra: Different Ways to Make Numbers

Draw the tens and ones.
Write the number in different ways.

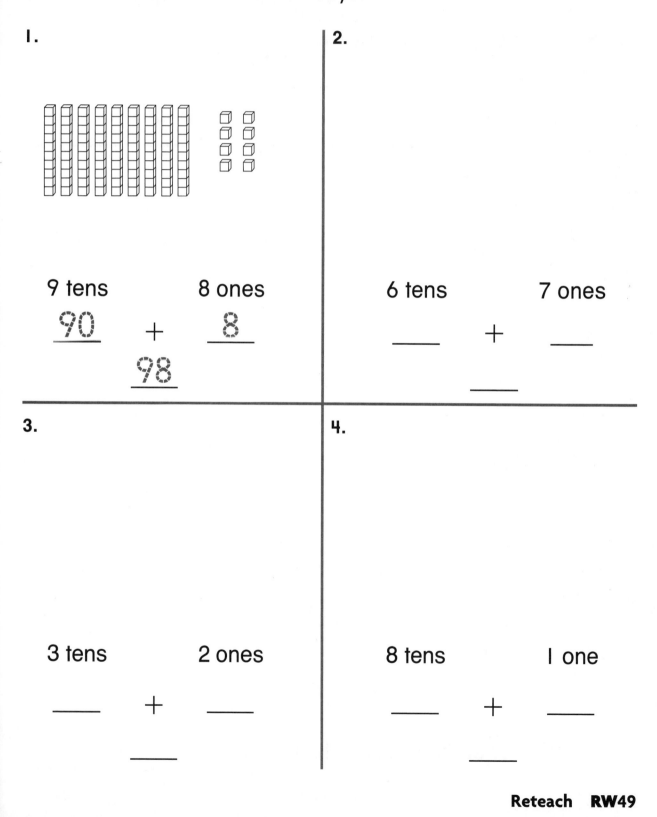

1.

9 tens   8 ones

_90_ + _8_

_98_

2.

6 tens   7 ones

___ + ___

___

3.

3 tens   2 ones

___ + ___

___

4.

8 tens   1 one

___ + ___

___

Problem Solving • Make Reasonable Estimates

About how many 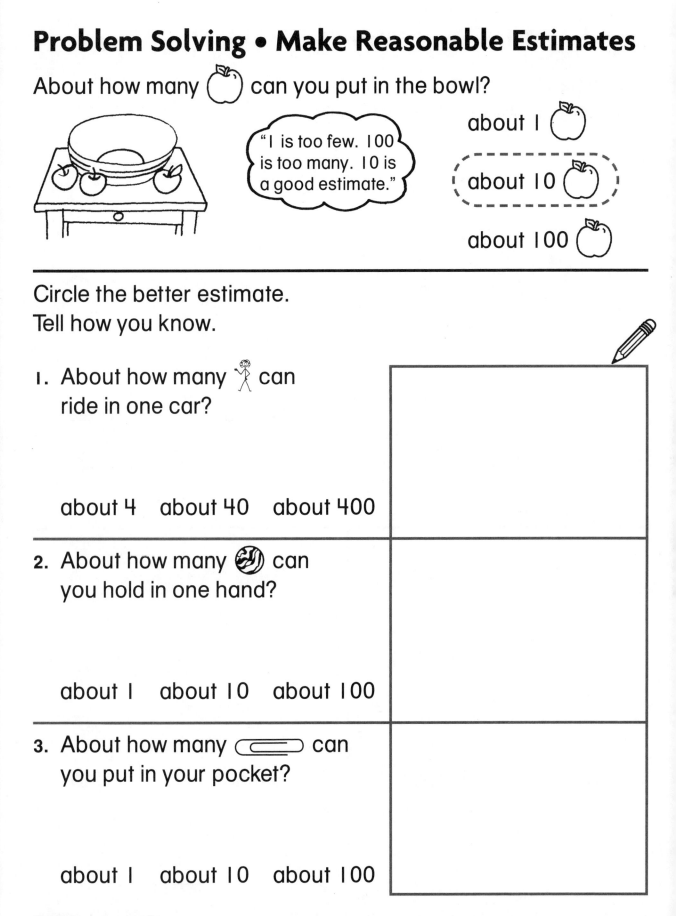 can you put in the bowl?

"I is too few. 100 is too many. 10 is a good estimate."

about 1

about 10

about 100

Circle the better estimate.
Tell how you know.

1. About how many ⚹ can ride in one car?

   about 4   about 40   about 400

2. About how many 🥐 can you hold in one hand?

   about 1   about 10   about 100

3. About how many ⚊ can you put in your pocket?

   about 1   about 10   about 100

Algebra: Greater Than

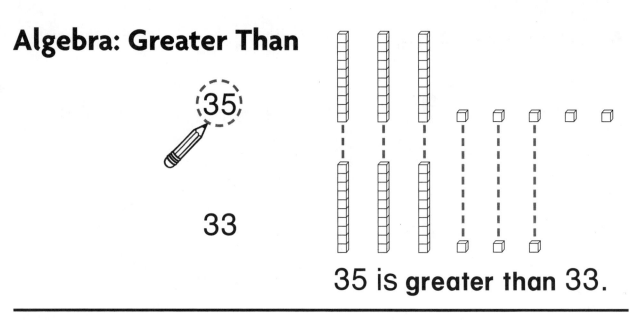

35

33

35 is **greater than** 33.

Draw lines to match.
Circle the greater number.

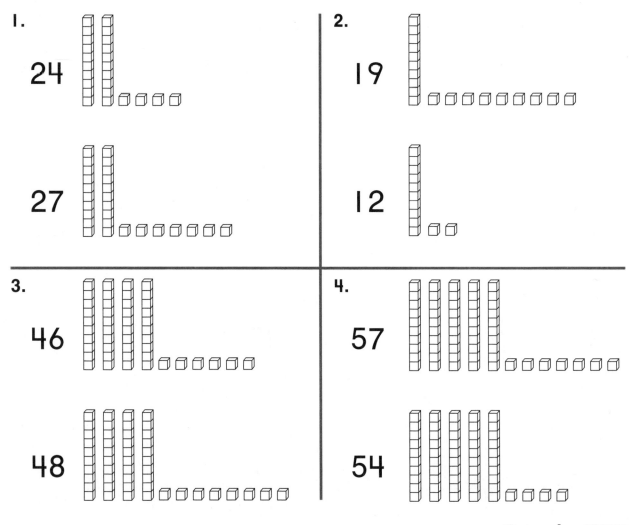

1.

24

27

2.

19

12

3.

46

48

4.

57

54

Algebra: Less Than

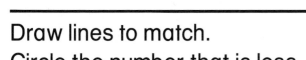

54

45 is **less than** 54.

Draw lines to match.
Circle the number that is less.

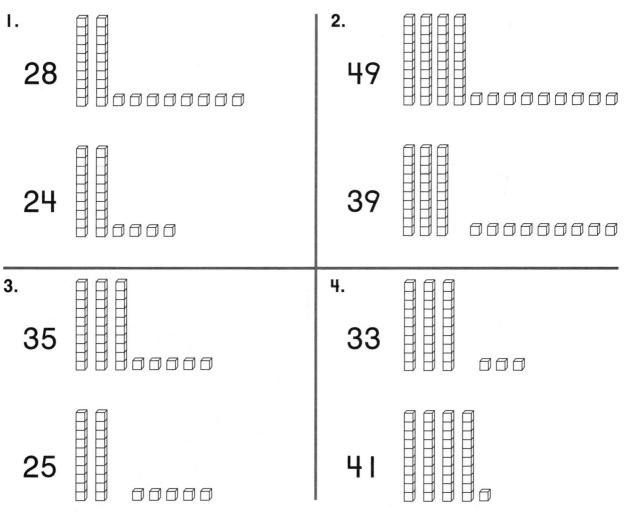

1.

28

24

2.

49

39

3.

35

25

4.

33

41

Algebra: Use Symbols to Compare

The mouth faces the greater number.

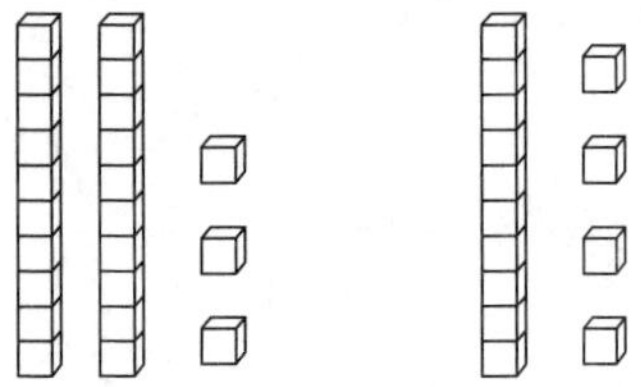

23    14
23 > 14
23 is greater than 14.

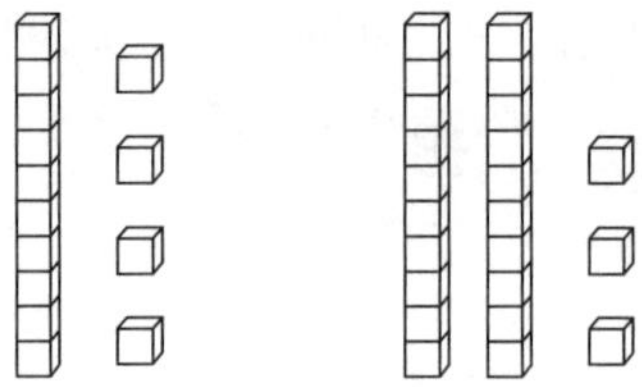

14    23
14 < 23
14 is less than 23.

Equal numbers use an equal sign.

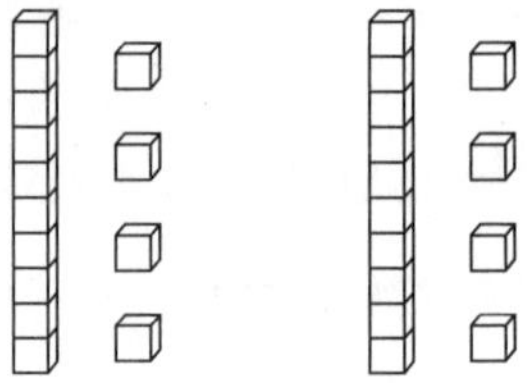

14 = 14
14 is equal to 14.

Write <, =, or >.

1.  32 > 23

2. 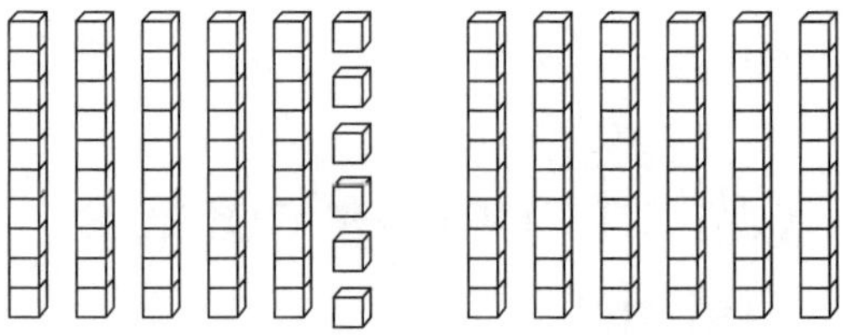 56 ☐ 60

3. 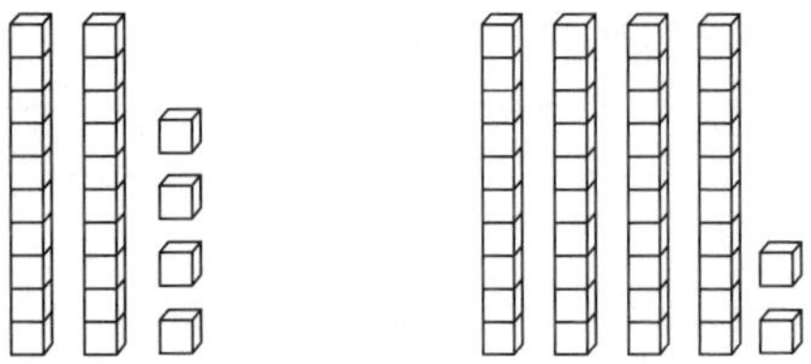 24 ☐ 42

4. 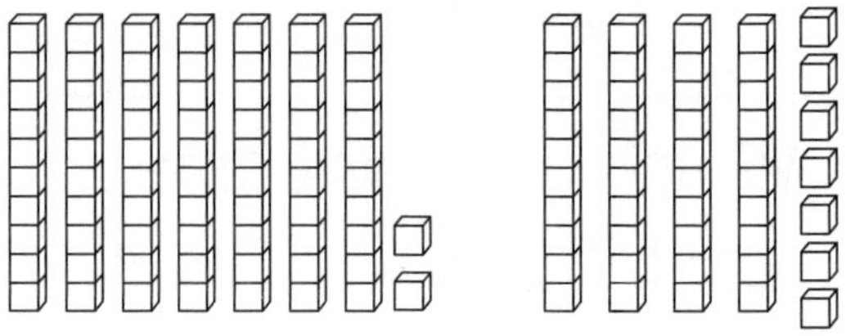 72 ☐ 47

5. 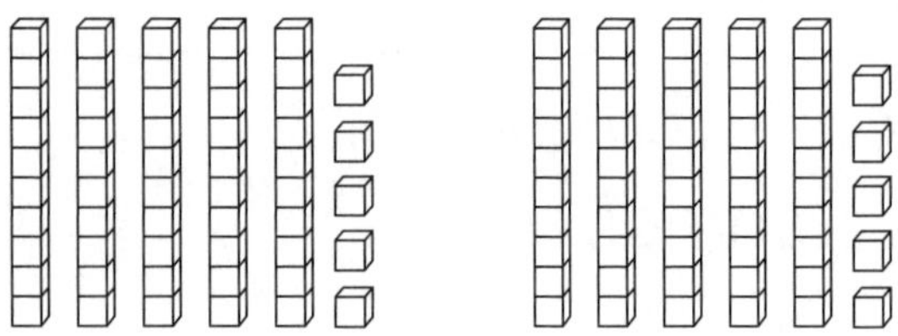 55 ☐ 55

6. 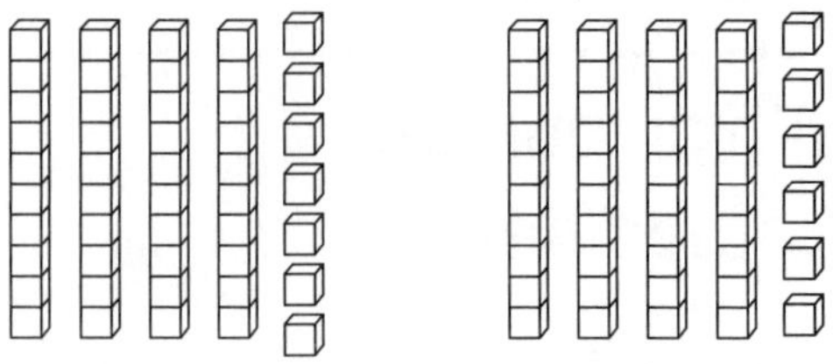 47 ☐ 46

Order on a Number Line

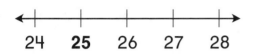

24 comes just **before** 25.
26 comes just **after** 25.
25 comes **between** 24 and 26.

Use the number line.
Write the number.

20 21 22 23 24 25 26 27 28 29 30 31 32 33 34 35

1. Which number comes just after?

   20, _2̲1̲_

2. Which number comes just after?

   34, ____

3. Which number comes just before?

   ____, 23

4. Which number comes just before?

   ____, 33

5. Which number comes between?

   33, ____, 35

6. Which number comes between?

   28, ____, 30

Count Forward and Backward

Count forward.

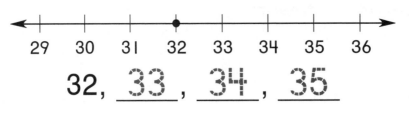

32, __33__, __34__, __35__

Count backward.

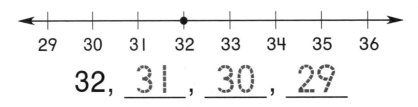

32, __31__, __30__, __29__

Count forward or backward.
Write the next three numbers.

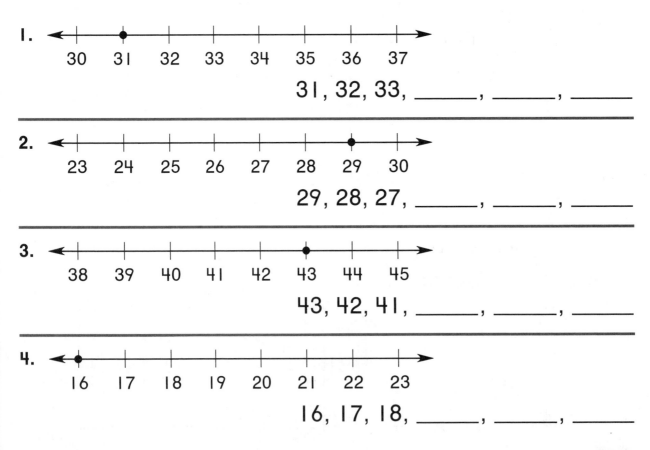

1.

30   31   32   33   34   35   36   37

31, 32, 33, _____, _____, _____

2.

23   24   25   26   27   28   29   30

29, 28, 27, _____, _____, _____

3.

38   39   40   41   42   43   44   45

43, 42, 41, _____, _____, _____

4.

16   17   18   19   20   21   22   23

16, 17, 18, _____, _____, _____

Name _____

Problem Solving • Use a Model

Use ⬚⬚⬚⬚⬚⬚ ⬚ .
Find 10 more or 10 fewer.
Write the numbers.

1. Rusty has 25 trucks.
   Jim has 10 more than Rusty.
   Tim has 10 fewer than Rusty.

   Tim has __15__ .   Rusty has 25.   Jim has __35__ .

2. Kira has 16 bows.
   Kim has 10 more than Kira.
   Kayla has 10 fewer than Kira.

   Kayla has _____.   Kira has _____.   Kim has _____.

3. Juan has 42 jacks.
   Lu has 10 more than Juan.
   Ali has 10 fewer than Juan.

   Ali has _____.   Juan has _____.   Lu has _____.

RW56   **Reteach**

Skip Count by 2s, 5s, and 10s

Count by twos.
Write how many.

> Add 2 to each number to get the next number.

1.

+2   +2

2 , _____ , _____

2.

+2   +2   +2

_____ , _____ , _____ , _____

Count by fives. Write how many.

> Add 5 to each number to get the next number.

3.

+5   +5   +5   +5   +5

5 , _____ , _____ , _____ , _____ , _____

4.

+5   +5   +5   +5   +5   +5

_____ , _____ , _____ , _____ , _____ , _____

Name _____

▶ LESSON 12.2

Algebra: Use a Hundred Chart to Skip Count

Count by tens. Write how many.

1.

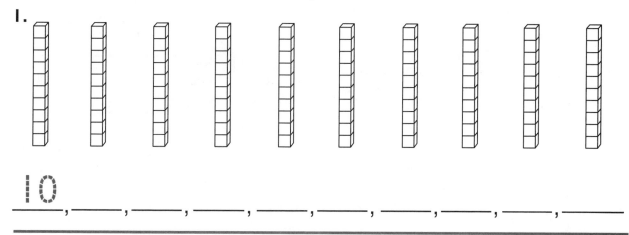

10 ____, ____, ____, ____, ____, ____, ____, ____, ____

2. Count by tens on the hundred chart. Write the numbers. Count by fives. Color the numbers.

1	2	3	4	5	6	7	8	9	
11	12	13	14	15	16	17	18	19	
21	22	23	24	25	26	27	28	29	
31	32	33	34	35	36	37	38	39	
41	42	43	44	45	46	47	48	49	
51	52	53	54	55	56	57	58	59	
61	62	63	64	65	66	67	68	69	
71	72	73	74	75	76	77	78	79	
81	82	83	84	85	86	87	88	89	
91	92	93	94	95	96	97	98	99	

Algebra: Patterns on a Hundred Chart

Start on 3. Count by 10s.
Start on 6. Count by 10s.
Start on 8. Count by 10s.
Write the missing numbers in the chart.

1	2	3	4	5	6	7	8	9	10
11	12	13	14	15	16	17		19	20
21	22	23	24	25		27		29	30
31	32		34	35		37		39	40
41	42		44	45		47		49	50
51	52		54	55		57		59	60
61	62		64	65		67		69	70
71	72		74	75		77		79	80
81	82		84	85		87		89	90
91	92		94	95		97		99	100

Even and Odd

Use 🎲 to show **even** and **odd** numbers.

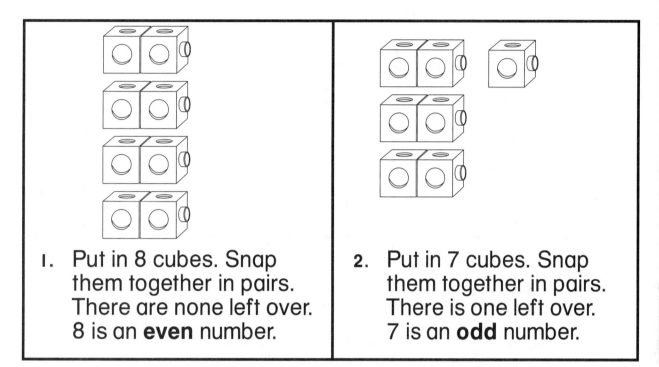

1. Put in 8 cubes. Snap them together in pairs. There are none left over. 8 is an **even** number.

2. Put in 7 cubes. Snap them together in pairs. There is one left over. 7 is an **odd** number.

Use cubes to show each number. Circle **even** or **odd**.

3. 9 even (odd)	4. 12 even odd
5. 2 even odd	6. 5 even odd
7. 13 even odd	8. 16 even odd
9. 6 even odd	10. 19 even odd

Problem Solving • Find a Pattern

Complete the chart.
Write the pattern.
Solve.

1.

number of starfish	1	2	3	4	5
number of arms	5	10			

Pattern: Count by ___fives___.

How many arms are on 5 starfish? __25__ arms

2.

number of mice	1	2	3	4	5
number of ears	2	4			

Pattern: Count by _____.

How many ears are on 5 mice? _____ ears

Ordinal Numbers

first second third fourth fifth sixth seventh eighth ninth tenth

Color to show the order.

1. first

2. second

3. third

4. fourth

5. fifth

6. sixth

7. seventh

8. eighth

9. ninth

10. tenth

Count On to Add

Count on to add. Write the numbers.
Write the sum.

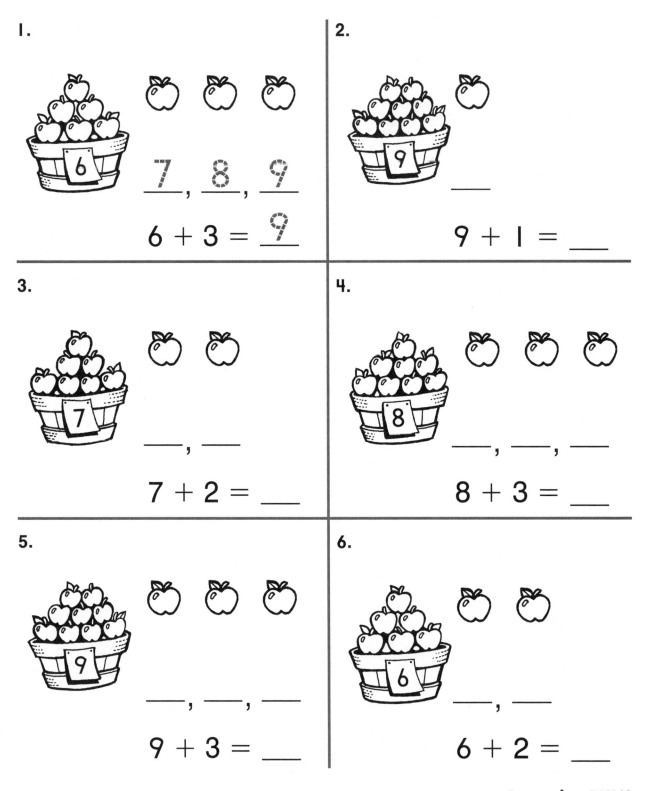

1.

6

7 , 8 , 9

6 + 3 = 9

2.

9

___

9 + 1 = ___

3.

7

___ , ___

7 + 2 = ___

4.

8

___ , ___ , ___

8 + 3 = ___

5.

9

___ , ___ , ___

9 + 3 = ___

6.

6

___ , ___

6 + 2 = ___

Name _____

Doubles and Doubles Plus 1

Use the pictures.
Complete the number sentence.

1.

$2 + \underline{2} = \underline{4}$

2.

$2 + \underline{} = \underline{}$

3.

$3 + \underline{} = \underline{}$

4.

$3 + \underline{} = \underline{}$

5.

$5 + \underline{} = \underline{}$

6.

$5 + \underline{} = \underline{}$

7.

$4 + \underline{} = \underline{}$

8.

$4 + \underline{} = \underline{}$

Algebra: Add 3 Numbers

Use cubes. Add the first two numbers.
Then add the third number.
Write the sum.

1.
$$\begin{array}{r} 4 \\ 1 \\ +2 \\ \hline \end{array}$$
$$\begin{array}{r} \boxed{5} \\ +2 \\ \hline 7 \end{array}$$

2.
$$\begin{array}{r} 3 \\ 3 \\ +4 \\ \hline \end{array}$$
$$\begin{array}{r} \square \\ +4 \\ \hline \end{array}$$

3.
$$\begin{array}{r} 2 \\ 6 \\ +2 \\ \hline \end{array}$$
$$\begin{array}{r} \square \\ +2 \\ \hline \end{array}$$

4.
$$\begin{array}{r} 2 \\ 2 \\ +2 \\ \hline \end{array}$$
$$\begin{array}{r} \square \\ +2 \\ \hline \end{array}$$

5.
$$\begin{array}{r} 9 \\ 2 \\ +1 \\ \hline \end{array}$$
$$\begin{array}{r} \square \\ +1 \\ \hline \end{array}$$

6.
$$\begin{array}{r} 1 \\ 3 \\ +4 \\ \hline \end{array}$$
$$\begin{array}{r} \square \\ +4 \\ \hline \end{array}$$

7.
$$\begin{array}{r} 6 \\ 1 \\ +2 \\ \hline \end{array}$$
$$\begin{array}{r} \square \\ +2 \\ \hline \end{array}$$

8.
$$\begin{array}{r} 4 \\ 4 \\ +3 \\ \hline \end{array}$$
$$\begin{array}{r} \square \\ +3 \\ \hline \end{array}$$

9.
$$\begin{array}{r} 1 \\ 2 \\ +3 \\ \hline \end{array}$$
$$\begin{array}{r} \square \\ +3 \\ \hline \end{array}$$

10.
$$\begin{array}{r} 4 \\ 2 \\ +3 \\ \hline \end{array}$$
$$\begin{array}{r} \square \\ +3 \\ \hline \end{array}$$

11.
$$\begin{array}{r} 3 \\ 3 \\ +3 \\ \hline \end{array}$$
$$\begin{array}{r} \square \\ +3 \\ \hline \end{array}$$

12.
$$\begin{array}{r} 1 \\ 1 \\ +5 \\ \hline \end{array}$$
$$\begin{array}{r} \square \\ +5 \\ \hline \end{array}$$

Problem Solving • Write a Number Sentence

Circle the number sentence that tells
about the story. Write the sum.

1. Shannon has 3 dolls.
   She finds 2 more.
   How many dolls does she
   have in all?

   $3 + 2 = \underline{5}$

   $2 + 2 = \underline{\hphantom{xx}}$

2. Michael picks 5 apples.
   Jill picks the same number.
   How many apples
   do they pick in all?

   $5 + 1 = \underline{\hphantom{xx}}$

   $5 + 5 = \underline{\hphantom{xx}}$

3. Claude reads 4 books.
   He reads 1 more.
   How many books does
   he read in all?

   $4 + 4 = \underline{\hphantom{xx}}$

   $4 + 1 = \underline{\hphantom{xx}}$

4. Ann found 4 rocks.
   Rachel found 5 rocks.
   How many rocks did they
   find in all?

   $4 + 5 = \underline{\hphantom{xx}}$

   $5 + 5 = \underline{\hphantom{xx}}$

5. Kara reads 6 pages
   in the morning.
   At night she reads 2 more.
   How many pages does she
   read in all?

   $6 + 3 = \underline{\hphantom{xx}}$

   $6 + 2 = \underline{\hphantom{xx}}$

Count Back to Subtract

Trace the arrows to count back.
Write the difference.

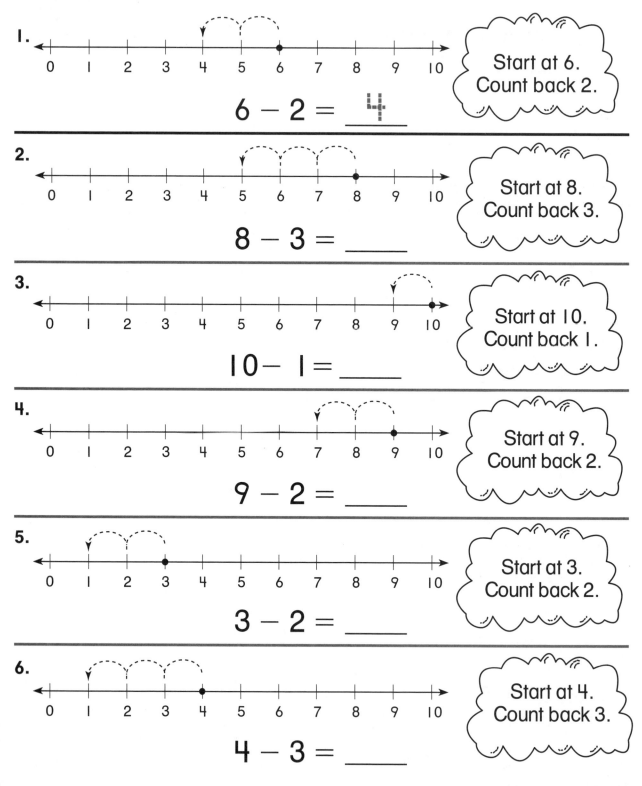

1.

$6 - 2 = \underline{4}$

Start at 6.
Count back 2.

2.

$8 - 3 = \underline{}$

Start at 8.
Count back 3.

3.

$10 - 1 = \underline{}$

Start at 10.
Count back 1.

4.

$9 - 2 = \underline{}$

Start at 9.
Count back 2.

5.

$3 - 2 = \underline{}$

Start at 3.
Count back 2.

6.

$4 - 3 = \underline{}$

Start at 4.
Count back 3.

Subtract to Compare

Draw lines to match. Subtract.
Write the difference.

These show the difference.

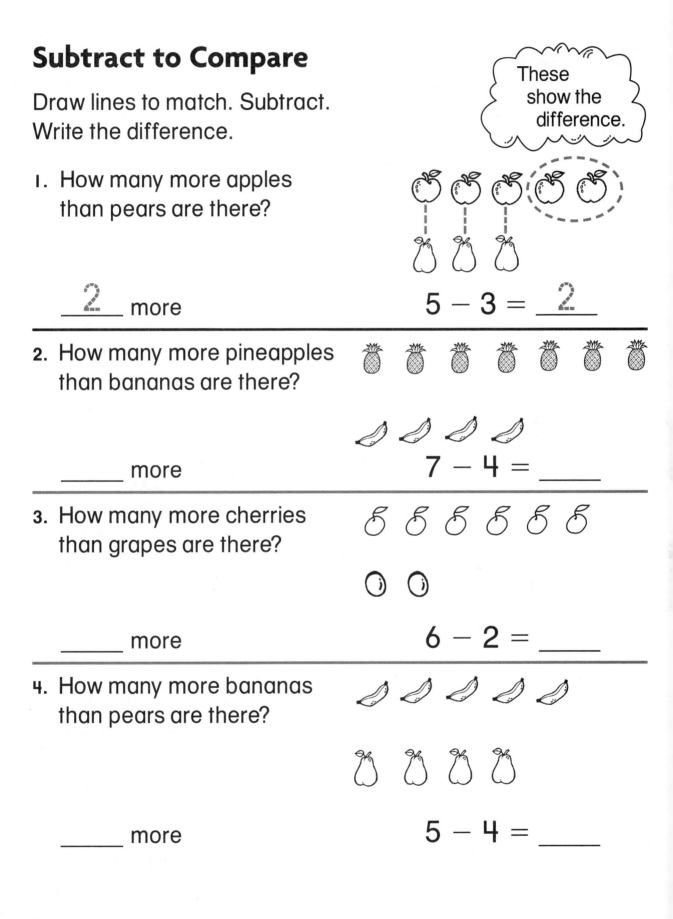

1. How many more apples than pears are there?

   __2__ more

   $5 - 3 = $ __2__

2. How many more pineapples than bananas are there?

   _____ more

   $7 - 4 = $ ____

3. How many more cherries than grapes are there?

   _____ more

   $6 - 2 = $ ____

4. How many more bananas than pears are there?

   _____ more

   $5 - 4 = $ ____

Algebra: Related Addition and Subtraction Facts

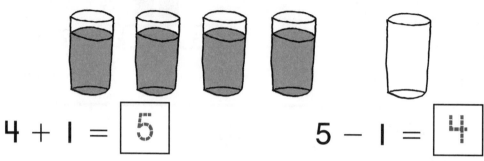

$4 + 1 =$ 5 $5 - 1 =$ 4

These facts are related. They use the same numbers.

Write the sum for the addition fact.
Then write the difference for the related subtraction fact.

1.

$2 + 4 = \boxed{}$ $6 - 4 = \boxed{}$

2.

$5 + 3 = \boxed{}$ $8 - 3 = \boxed{}$

3.

$2 + 5 = \boxed{}$ $7 - 5 = \boxed{}$

4.

$7 + 3 = \boxed{}$ $10 - 3 = \boxed{}$

5.

$2 + 1 = \boxed{}$ $3 - 1 = \boxed{}$

6.

$4 + 5 = \boxed{}$ $9 - 5 = \boxed{}$

Fact Families to 12

These facts are in the same **fact family**. They all use the same numbers.

$2 + 5 = 7$ $7 - 5 = 2$

$5 + 2 = 7$ $7 - 2 = 5$

Add or subtract. Write the missing numbers.
Use the first fact to help you.

1. $1 + 3 = 4$ $4 - 3 = \underline{1}$

   $3 + 1 = \underline{4}$ $4 - 1 = \underline{3}$

---

2. $3 + 2 = 5$ $5 - 2 = \underline{}$

   $2 + 3 = \underline{}$ $5 - 3 = \underline{}$

---

3. $4 + 3 = 7$ $7 - 3 = \underline{}$

   $3 + 4 = \underline{}$ $7 - 4 = \underline{}$

---

4. $2 + 4 = 6$ $6 - 4 = \underline{}$

   $4 + 2 = \underline{}$ $6 - 2 = \underline{}$

---

5. $5 + 4 = 9$ $9 - 4 = \underline{}$

   $4 + 5 = \underline{}$ $9 - 5 = \underline{}$

Name _____

Sums and Differences to 12

Circle the best way to solve each group. Then write each sum or difference.

Count on to solve all these problems.
$8 + 2 = \underline{10}$
$10 + 1 = \underline{11}$
$5 + 3 = \underline{8}$

1. How can you solve these problems?

count on   use doubles
(count back)   use related facts

$5 - 1 = \underline{4}$
$10 - 2 = \underline{8}$
$12 - 3 = \underline{9}$

2. How can you solve these problems?

count on   use doubles
count back   use related facts

$6 + 4 = \underline{}$
$4 + 6 = \underline{}$
$10 - 4 = \underline{}$

3. How can you solve these problems?

count on   use doubles
count back   use related facts

$5 + 5 = \underline{}$
$6 + 6 = \underline{}$
$3 + 3 = \underline{}$

4. How can you solve these problems?

count on   use doubles
count back   use related facts

$2 + 1 = \underline{}$
$1 + 2 = \underline{}$
$7 + 3 = \underline{}$

Algebra: Missing Numbers

Write the missing number.
Use 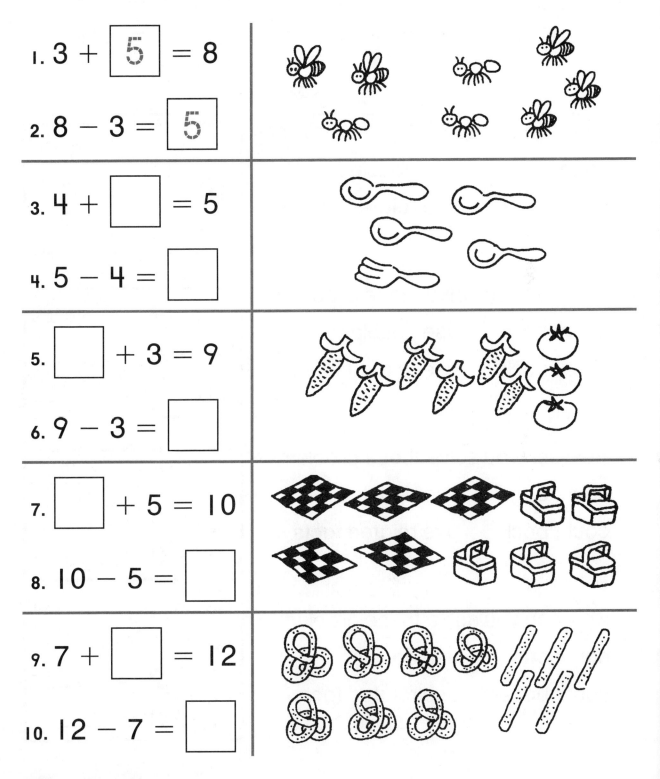 if you need to.

1. $3 + \boxed{5} = 8$

2. $8 - 3 = \boxed{5}$

3. $4 + \boxed{} = 5$

4. $5 - 4 = \boxed{}$

5. $\boxed{} + 3 = 9$

6. $9 - 3 = \boxed{}$

7. $\boxed{} + 5 = 10$

8. $10 - 5 = \boxed{}$

9. $7 + \boxed{} = 12$

10. $12 - 7 = \boxed{}$

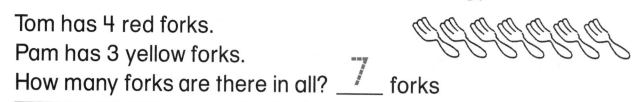
Problem Solving • Choose a Strategy

Tom has 4 red forks.
Pam has 3 yellow forks.
How many forks are there in all? __7__ forks

Draw a line to show how to solve each problem.

1. Annie has 6 strawberries.
   She eats 3 of them.
   How many strawberries are left?

2. Ray has 7 sandwiches.
   Mark has 3 sandwiches.
   How many sandwiches are there in all?

3. Peter has 10 cherries.
   He eats 5 of them.
   How many cherries
   are left?

4. Beth has 7 apples.
   She gives away 3 apples.
   How many apples does she have left?

5. Choose one of the problems above.
   Show a different way to solve it.
   Write the number sentence.

   ____ ◯ ____ ◯ ____

Solid Figures

Use solids.

1. Circle the solids that slide.

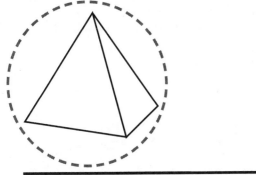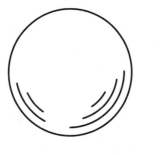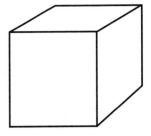

2. Circle the solids that stack.

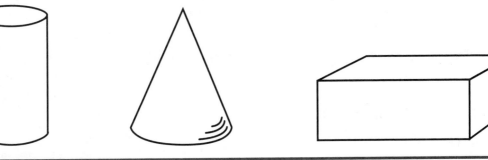

3. Circle the solids that roll.

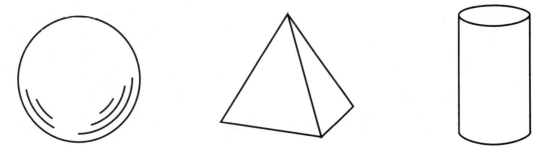

4. Circle the solids that slide.

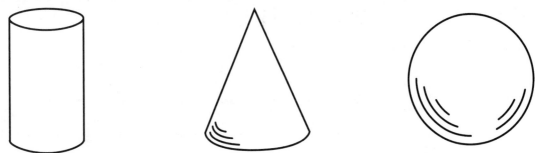

Faces and Vertices

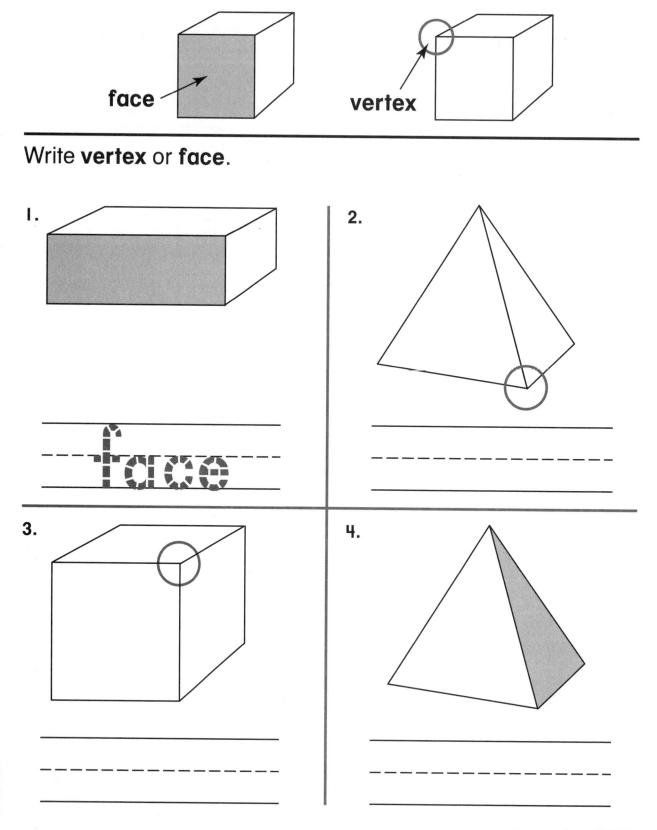

face

vertex

Write **vertex** or **face**.

1.

face

2.

3.

4.

Plane Shapes on Solid Figures

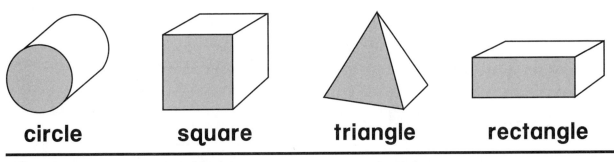

circle   square   triangle   rectangle

Color the shape that matches the face of the solid.

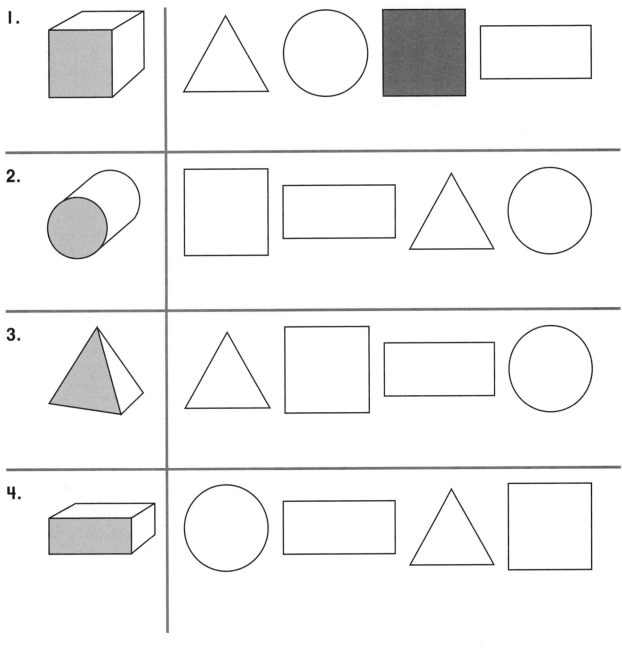

1.

2.

3.

4.

Sort and Identify Plane Shapes

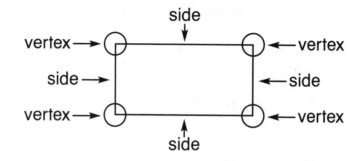

This shape has 4 **sides** and 4 **vertices.**

Trace the shapes.

1. Circle the shape with 3 sides and 3 vertices.

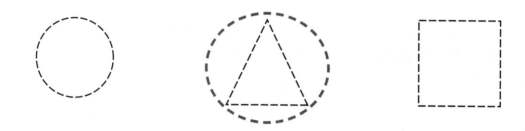

2. Circle the shape with 4 sides and 4 vertices.

3. Circle the shape with 0 vertices.

Problem Solving • Make a Model

What shape can you make with two △?

Use pattern blocks to solve.
Draw the new shape you make.

1. What can you make with two ▢?	
2. What can you make with two ⬯?	
3. What can you make with three △?	
4. What can you make with two △ and two ◇?	

Open and Closed

Is the first figure open or closed?
Circle the figure that is the same.

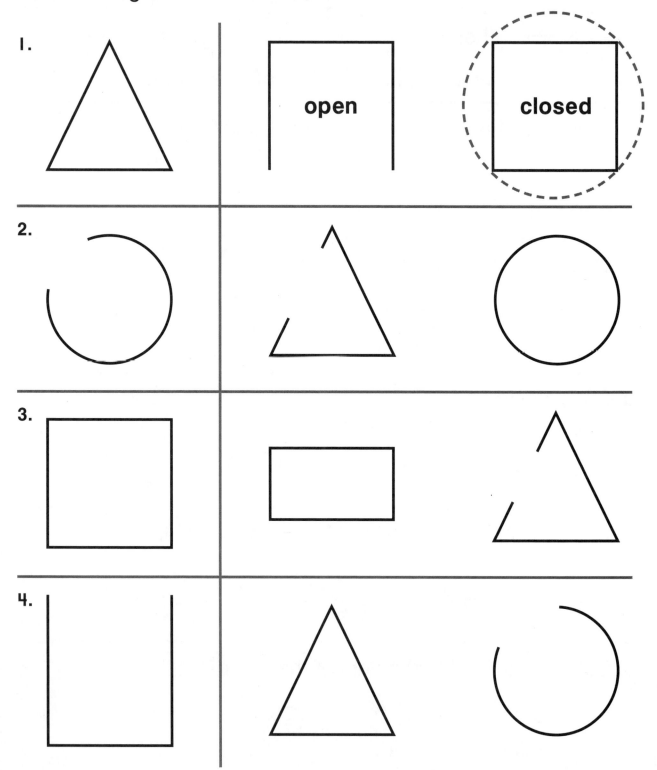

Name ____

Problem Solving • Use a Picture

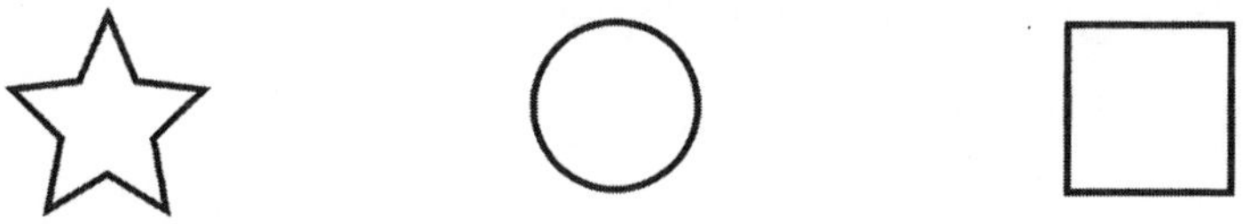

← Left Right →

The star is to the left of the circle.

---

1. Color the shape to the right of the □ [orange].

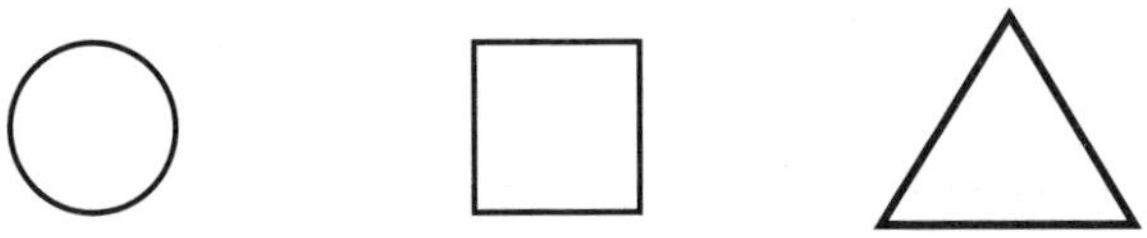

---

2. Color the shape to the right of the ☆ [blue].

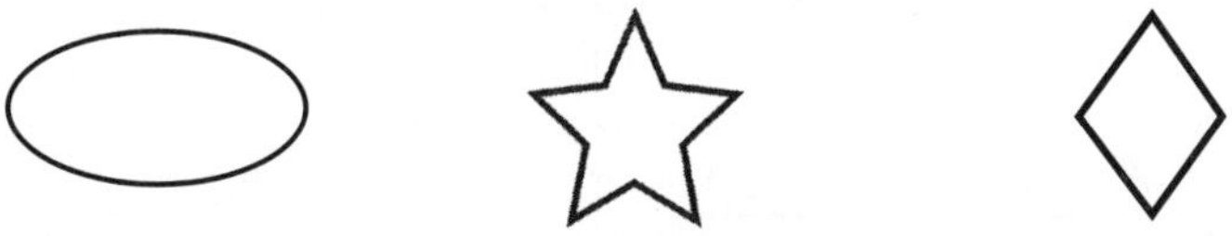

---

3. Color the animal to the right of the pig [yellow].

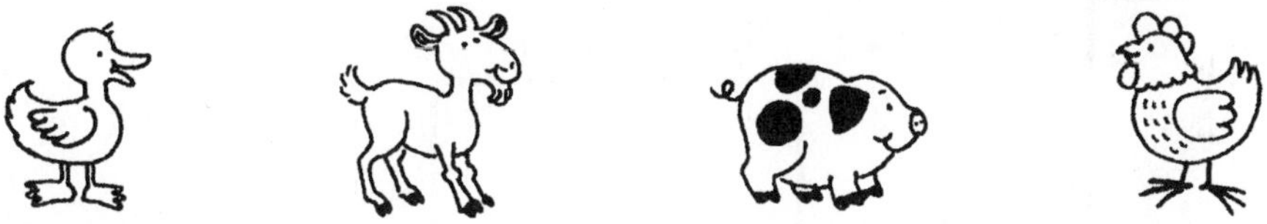

---

4. Color the animal to the left of the turtle [green].

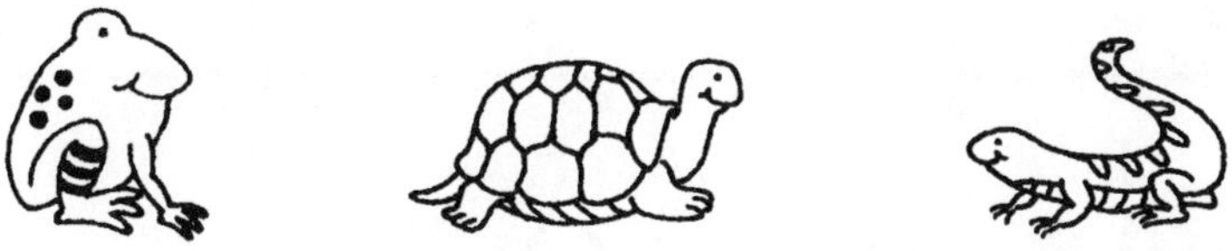

---

5. Color the animal to the right of the rabbit [brown].

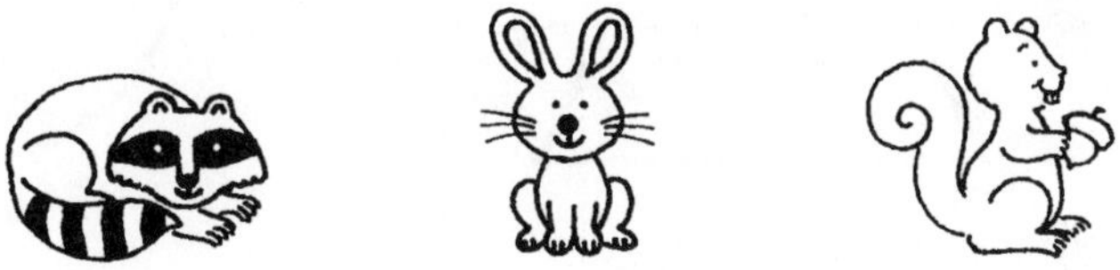

Give and Follow Directions

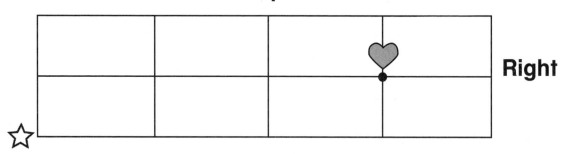

The heart is 3 spaces to the right
of the star and 1 space up.

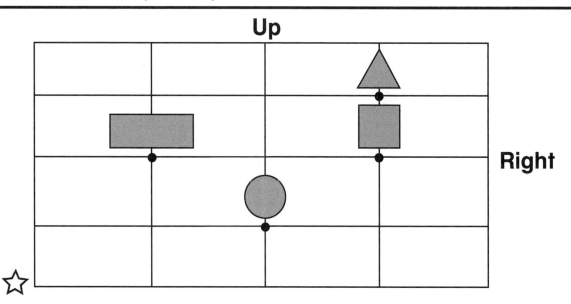

Start at ☆. Follow the directions.
Draw the shape.

1. Go 1 space to the right and 2 spaces up.   _____

2. Go 3 spaces to the right and 2 spaces up.   _____

3. Go 2 spaces to the right and 1 space up.   _____

4. Go 3 spaces to the right and 3 spaces up.   _____

Symmetry

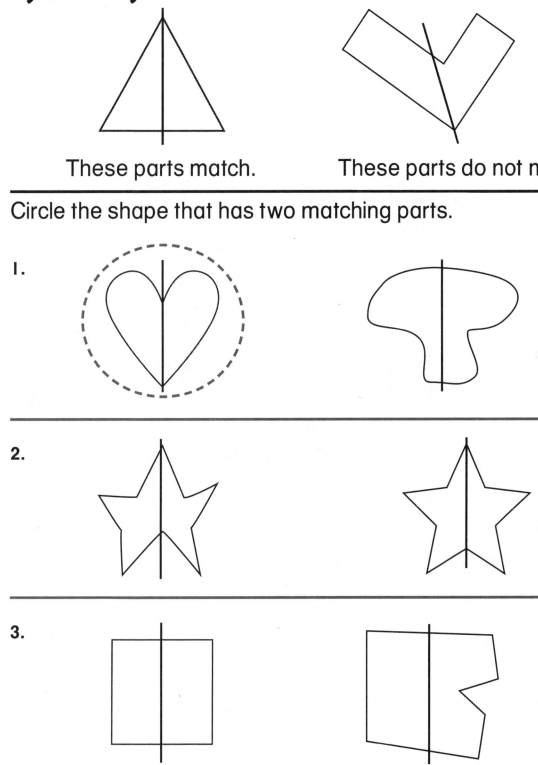

These parts match.   These parts do not match.

Circle the shape that has two matching parts.

1.

2.

3.

Slides and Turns

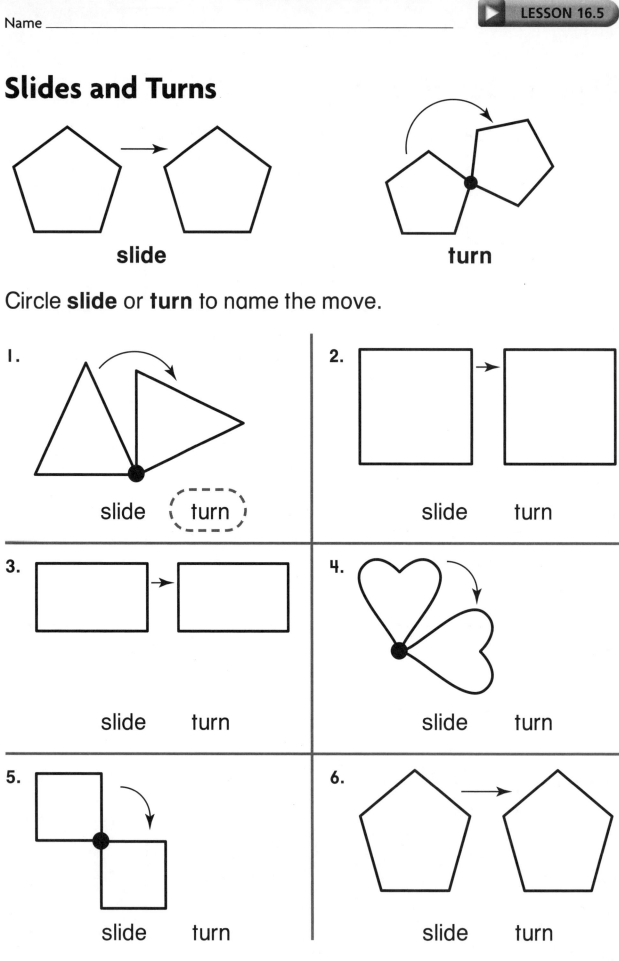

slide   **turn**

Circle **slide** or **turn** to name the move.

1.

slide   (turn)

2.

slide   turn

3.

slide   turn

4.

slide   turn

5.

slide   turn

6.

slide   turn

Algebra: Describe and Extend Patterns

Circle the shape that comes next in the pattern.

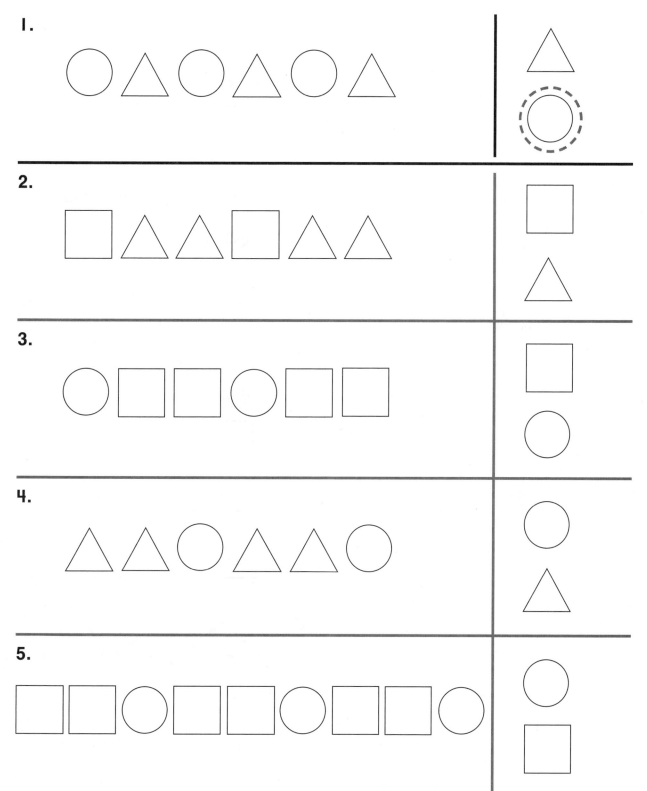

Algebra: Pattern Units

Color the squares to continue the pattern.
Circle the pattern unit.

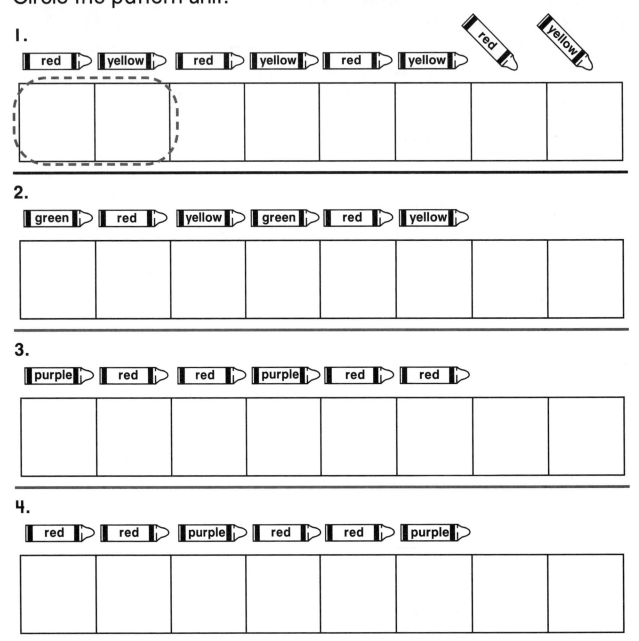

1.

red ▷ yellow ▷ red ▷ yellow ▷ red ▷ yellow ▷ red ▷ yellow ▷

2.

green ▷ red ▷ yellow ▷ green ▷ red ▷ yellow ▷

3.

purple ▷ red ▷ red ▷ purple ▷ red ▷ red ▷

4.

red ▷ red ▷ purple ▷ red ▷ red ▷ purple ▷

Algebra: Make New Patterns

Use shapes to continue the pattern.
Then use the same shapes to make a different pattern.
Draw your new pattern.

1.

2.

3.

4.

Problem Solving • Correct a Pattern

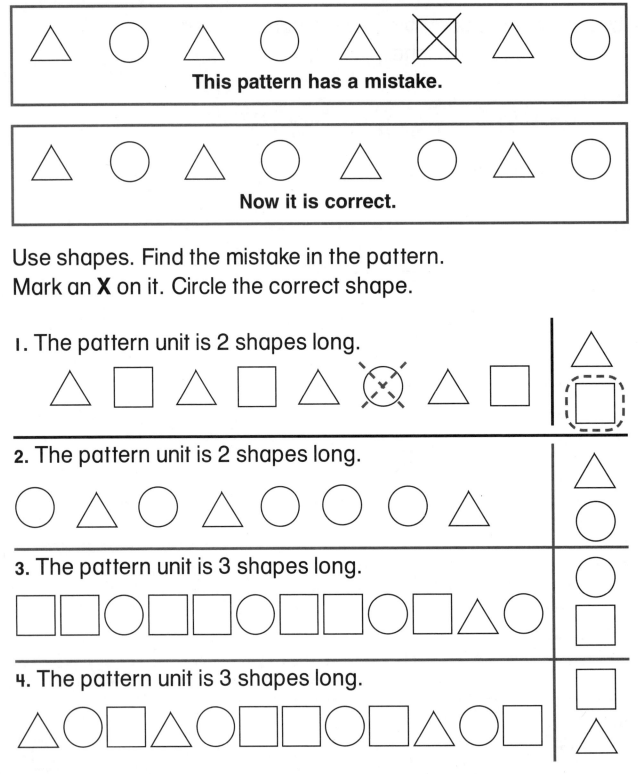

This pattern has a mistake.

Now it is correct.

Use shapes. Find the mistake in the pattern.
Mark an **X** on it. Circle the correct shape.

1. The pattern unit is 2 shapes long.

2. The pattern unit is 2 shapes long.

3. The pattern unit is 3 shapes long.

4. The pattern unit is 3 shapes long.

Problem Solving • Transfer Patterns

Use different colors to show the same pattern.
Color the shapes.

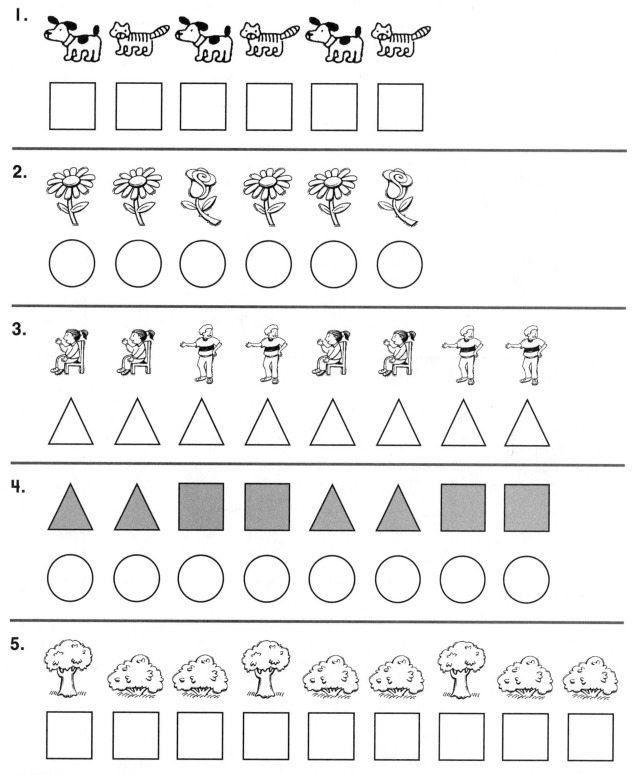

RW88   Reteach

Doubles and Doubles Plus 1

Doubles		Doubles Plus One	
6 + 6 ――― 12	♡♡♡♡♡♡ ♥♥♥♥♥♥	6 + 7 ――― 13	♡♡♡♡♡♡ ♥♥♥♥♥♥♥

Use doubles. Add 1.

Add. Then add one more.

1.
5 + 5 ―― 10	☆☆☆☆☆ ★★★★★	5 + 6 ―― 11	☆☆☆☆☆ ★★★★★★

2.
9 + 9	△△△△△△△△△ ▲▲▲▲▲▲▲▲▲	9 +10	△△△△△△△△△ ▲▲▲▲▲▲▲▲▲▲

3.
7 + 7	○○○○○○○ ●●●●●●●	7 + 8	○○○○○○○ ●●●●●●●●

4.
4 + 4	◇◇◇◇ ◆◆◆◆	4 + 5	◇◇◇◇ ◆◆◆◆◆

5.
8 + 8	☐☐☐☐☐☐☐☐ ■■■■■■■■	8 + 9	☐☐☐☐☐☐☐☐ ■■■■■■■■■

Name _____

10 and More

You can use ● and Workmat 7 to add.

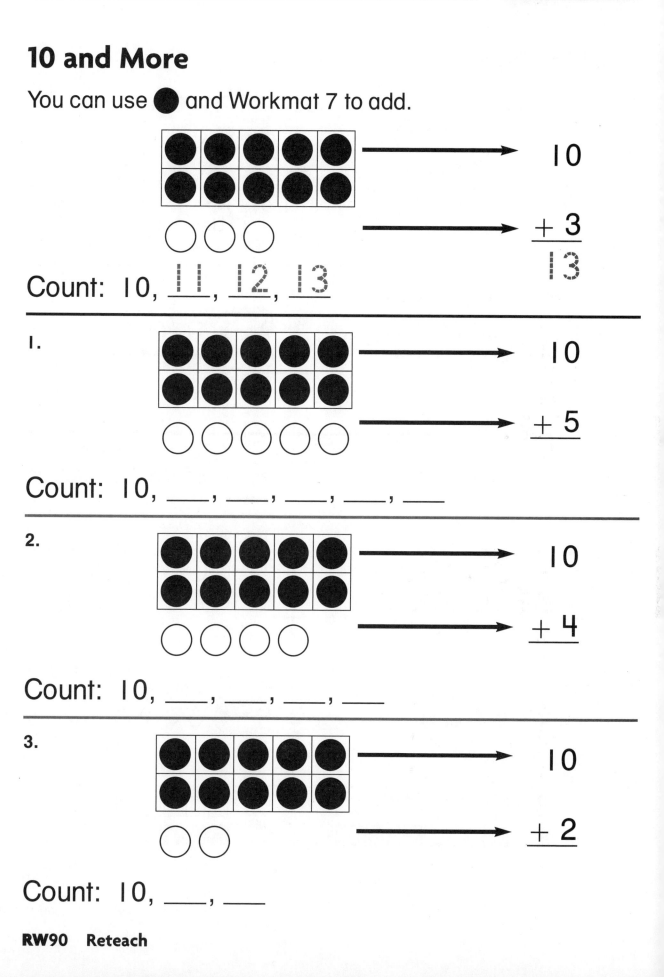

⟶ 10

⟶ $\begin{array}{r} + 3 \\ \hline 13 \end{array}$

Count: 10, __11__, __12__, __13__

1.

⟶ 10

⟶ $+ 5$

Count: 10, ____, ____, ____, ____, ____

2.

⟶ 10

⟶ $+ 4$

Count: 10, ____, ____, ____, ____

3.

⟶ 10

⟶ $+ 2$

Count: 10, ____, ____

Make 10 to Add

Use ⬤ and Workmat 7 to add.
Write the sums.

1. Show 9. Show 6.   Make a ten.

$$9 + 6 = 10 + 5$$

$$\begin{array}{r} 9 \\ + 6 \\ \hline 15 \end{array} \qquad \begin{array}{r} 10 \\ + 5 \\ \hline 15 \end{array}$$

2. Show 9. Show 4.   Make a ten.

$$9 + 4 = 10 + 3$$

$$\begin{array}{r} 9 \\ + 4 \\ \hline \end{array} \qquad \begin{array}{r} 10 \\ + 3 \\ \hline \end{array}$$

3. Show 9. Show 7.   Make a ten.

$$9 + 7 = 10 + 6$$

$$\begin{array}{r} 9 \\ + 7 \\ \hline \end{array} \qquad \begin{array}{r} 10 \\ + 6 \\ \hline \end{array}$$

4. Show 9. Show 5.   Make a ten.

$$9 + 5 = 10 + 4$$

$$\begin{array}{r} 9 \\ + 5 \\ \hline \end{array} \qquad \begin{array}{r} 10 \\ + 4 \\ \hline \end{array}$$

Use Make a 10

Use ● and Workmat 7 to add. Write the missing number. Write the sums.

1. Show 8. Show 4.   Make a ten.

$$8 + 4 \qquad = \qquad 10 + \underline{2}$$

$$\begin{array}{r} 8 \\ + 4 \\ \hline 12 \end{array} \qquad \begin{array}{r} 10 \\ + 2 \\ \hline 12 \end{array}$$

2. Show 7. Show 6.   Make a ten.

$$7 + 6 \qquad = \qquad 10 + \underline{}$$

$$\begin{array}{r} 7 \\ + 6 \\ \hline \end{array} \qquad \begin{array}{r} 10 \\ + \\ \hline \end{array}$$

3. Show 8. Show 7.   Make a ten.

$$8 + 7 \qquad = \qquad 10 + \underline{}$$

$$\begin{array}{r} 8 \\ + 7 \\ \hline \end{array} \qquad \begin{array}{r} 10 \\ + \\ \hline \end{array}$$

4. Show 6. Show 5.   Make a ten.

$$6 + 5 \qquad = \qquad 10 + \underline{}$$

$$\begin{array}{r} 6 \\ + 5 \\ \hline \end{array} \qquad \begin{array}{r} 10 \\ + \\ \hline \end{array}$$

Algebra: Add 3 Numbers

Use doubles or make a ten to add.
Then add again.

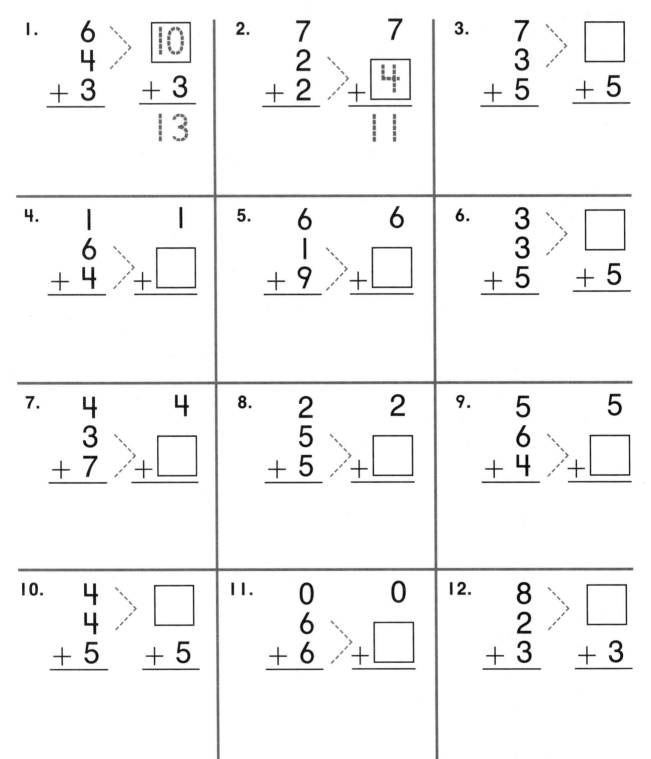

1. 6
    4
    + 3   + 3

             13

2. 7   7
    2
    + 2   + 4

          11

3. 7   ☐
    3
    + 5   + 5

4. 1   1
    6
    + 4   + ☐

5. 6   6
    1
    + 9   + ☐

6. 3   ☐
    3
    + 5   + 5

7. 4   4
    3
    + 7   + ☐

8. 2   2
    5
    + 5   + ☐

9. 5   5
    6
    + 4   + ☐

10. 4   ☐
    4
    + 5   + 5

11. 0   0
    6
    + 6   + ☐

12. 8   ☐
    2
    + 3   + 3

Problem Solving • Use Data from a Table

This table tells how many animals
children saw at the lake.

Animals	Number
turtle	6
fish	2
frog	4
snake	5

Use the table to answer the questions.

1. How many animals were fish or frogs?

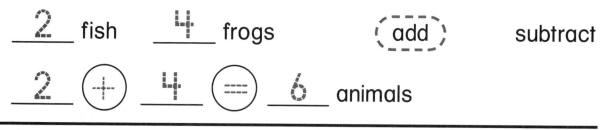

___2___ fish   ___4___ frogs   (add)   subtract

___2___ (+) ___4___ (=) ___6___ animals

_____

2. How many more snakes than fish did they see?

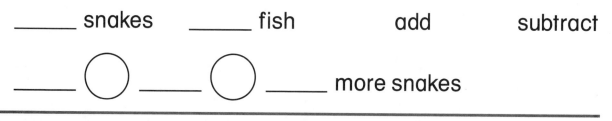

_____ snakes   _____ fish   add   subtract

_____ ◯ _____ ◯ _____ more snakes

_____

3. How many animals were not fish or frogs?

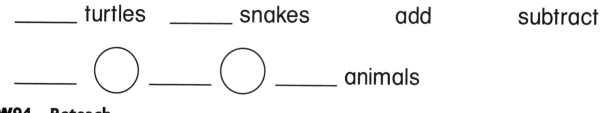

_____ turtles   _____ snakes   add   subtract

_____ ◯ _____ ◯ _____ animals

Use a Number Line to Count Back

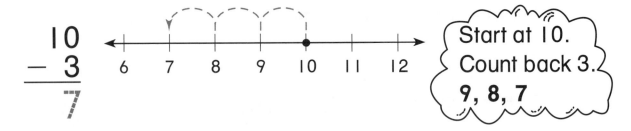

$$10 - 3 = 7$$

Start at 10.
Count back 3.
9, 8, 7

Count back to subtract. Write the difference.
Use the number line to help.

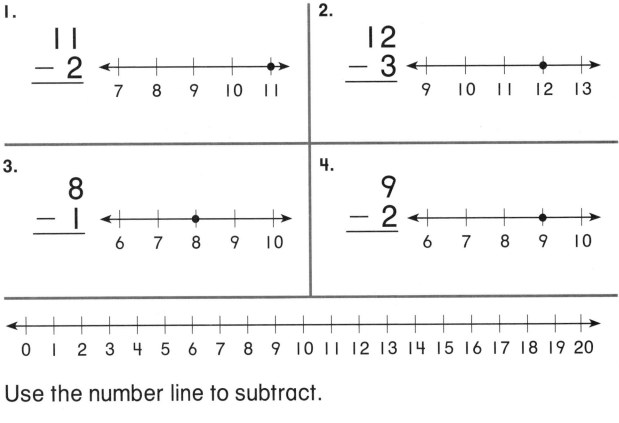

1.
$$11 - 2$$

2.
$$12 - 3$$

3.
$$8 - 1$$

4.
$$9 - 2$$

Use the number line to subtract.

5. $$16 - 7$$

6. $$20 - 3$$

7. $$12 - 5$$

8. $$18 - 9$$

Doubles Fact Families

Use 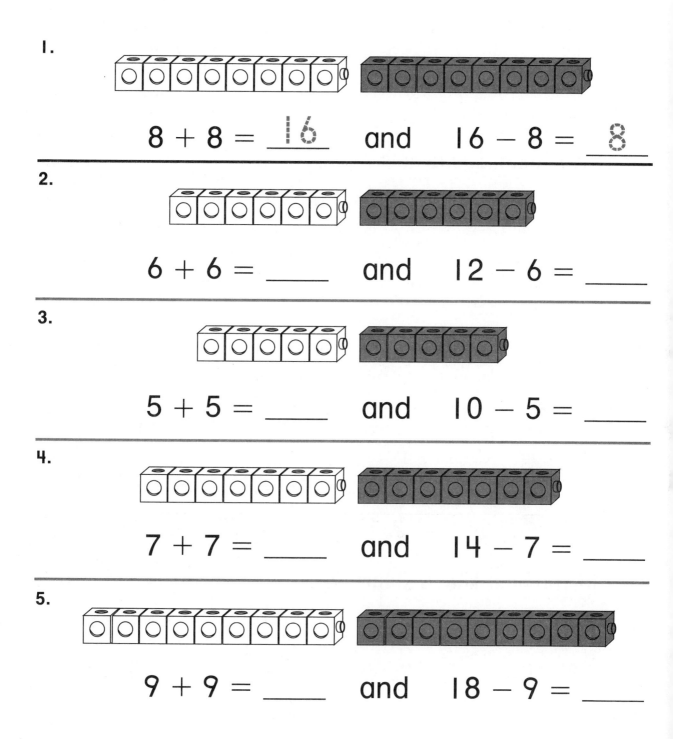. Write the sum and difference for each pair.

1.

$8 + 8 = \underline{16}$ and $16 - 8 = \underline{8}$

2.

$6 + 6 = \underline{\hphantom{00}}$ and $12 - 6 = \underline{\hphantom{00}}$

3.

$5 + 5 = \underline{\hphantom{00}}$ and $10 - 5 = \underline{\hphantom{00}}$

4.

$7 + 7 = \underline{\hphantom{00}}$ and $14 - 7 = \underline{\hphantom{00}}$

5.

$9 + 9 = \underline{\hphantom{00}}$ and $18 - 9 = \underline{\hphantom{00}}$

Name _____

Algebra: Related Addition and Subtraction Facts

Add. Then cross out marbles to subtract.

$$\begin{array}{r} 8 \\ +\ 7 \\ \hline 15 \end{array}$$

$$\begin{array}{r} 15 \\ -\ 7 \\ \hline 8 \end{array}$$

Add. Put the groups together.

Subtract. Cross out to take away.

1.
$$\begin{array}{r} 9 \\ +\ 8 \\ \hline \end{array}$$

$$\begin{array}{r} 17 \\ -\ 8 \\ \hline \end{array}$$

2.
$$\begin{array}{r} 8 \\ +\ 8 \\ \hline \end{array}$$

$$\begin{array}{r} 16 \\ -\ 8 \\ \hline \end{array}$$

3.
$$\begin{array}{r} 9 \\ +\ 7 \\ \hline \end{array}$$

$$\begin{array}{r} 16 \\ -\ 7 \\ \hline \end{array}$$

4.
$$\begin{array}{r} 9 \\ +\ 3 \\ \hline \end{array}$$

$$\begin{array}{r} 12 \\ -\ 3 \\ \hline \end{array}$$

Problem Solving • Estimate Reasonable Answers

Greg has 4 pumpkins.
Carol has 5 pumpkins.
About how many pumpkins
do they have in all?

about ___10___ pumpkins

THINK
The sum of 4 + 5 is 9.
9 is close to 10.

Estimate the answer.
Write 5, 10, 15, or 20.

1. Donna picks 9 flowers.
   Carol picks 3 flowers.
   About how many more flowers
   does Donna pick?

   about _____ more flowers

---

2. Tara has 3 seeds.
   She needs 12 in all.
   About how many more seeds
   does she need?

   about _____ more seeds

---

3. Tariq plants 11 rows of corn.
   Then he plants 8 more.
   About how many
   rows of corn does he plant?

   about _____ rows

---

4. 9 children pick strawberries.
   Then 7 more join them.
   About how many children
   pick strawberries?

   about _____ children

Practice the Facts

Add. Then cross out marbles to subtract.

1. 8
   + 3

2. 11
   − 3

3. 8
   + 6

4. 14
   − 6

Find the sum or difference.
Use one fact to help you solve the other.

5. 10 − 1 = ___ , so 9 + 1 = ___

6. 5 + 5 = ___ , so 6 + 5 = ___

7. 6 + 6 = ___ , so 6 + 7 = ___

8. 9 + 9 = ___ , so 18 − 9 = ___

Fact Families to 20

Write the sums and differences
for each fact family.

1. $7 + 4 = \underline{11}$

   $4 + 7 = \underline{11}$

   $11 - 7 = \underline{4}$

   $11 - 4 = \underline{7}$

2. $8 + 5 = \underline{}$

   $5 + 8 = \underline{}$

   $13 - 8 = \underline{}$

   $13 - 5 = \underline{}$

3. $9 + 3 = \underline{}$

   $3 + 9 = \underline{}$

   $12 - 9 = \underline{}$

   $12 - 3 = \underline{}$

4. $8 + 7 = \underline{}$

   $7 + 8 = \underline{}$

   $15 - 8 = \underline{}$

   $15 - 7 = \underline{}$

5. $9 + 8 = \underline{}$

   $8 + 9 = \underline{}$

   $17 - 9 = \underline{}$

   $17 - 8 = \underline{}$

6. $9 + 5 = \underline{}$

   $5 + 9 = \underline{}$

   $14 - 9 = \underline{}$

   $14 - 5 = \underline{}$

RW100 Reteach

Algebra: Ways to Make Numbers to 20

Put an X on the way that does **not** make the number.

1. | 19 | $10 + 9$ | $19 - 0$ | $1 + 8 + 9$ | $3 + 7 + 9$

2. | 18 | $18 - 0$ | $3 + 4 + 9$ | $10 + 8$ | $6 + 3 + 9$

3. | 15 | $7 + 3 + 5$ | $8 + 7$ | $6 + 3 + 6$ | $4 + 2 + 10$

4. | 13 | $6 + 7$ | $1 + 7 + 5$ | $10 - 3$ | $4 + 5 + 4$

5. | 17 | $9 + 8$ | $6 + 3 + 5$ | $3 + 4 + 10$ | $10 + 7$

6. | 16 | $7 + 9$ | $9 + 9$ | $8 + 8$ | $5 + 5 + 6$

7. | 12 | $6 + 4 + 2$ | $5 + 4 + 4$ | $7 + 5$ | $1 + 6 + 5$

8. | 14 | $3 + 5 + 7$ | $3 + 4 + 7$ | $3 + 3 + 8$ | $8 + 6$

Problem Solving • Make a Model

Match each problem to a model.
Then solve.

1. 8 penguins swim.
   6 more join them.
   How many penguins
   are there now?

   __14__ penguins

2. Tad has 4 snowballs.
   Pat has 11 snowballs.
   How many more does
   Pat have than Tad?

   _____ snowballs

3. 10 friends play in the snow.
   5 other friends make a snowman.
   How many friends are there
   in all?

   _____ friends

4. Paul needs 12 hats.
   He has 8 hats.
   How many more hats
   does he need?

   _____ hats

Halves

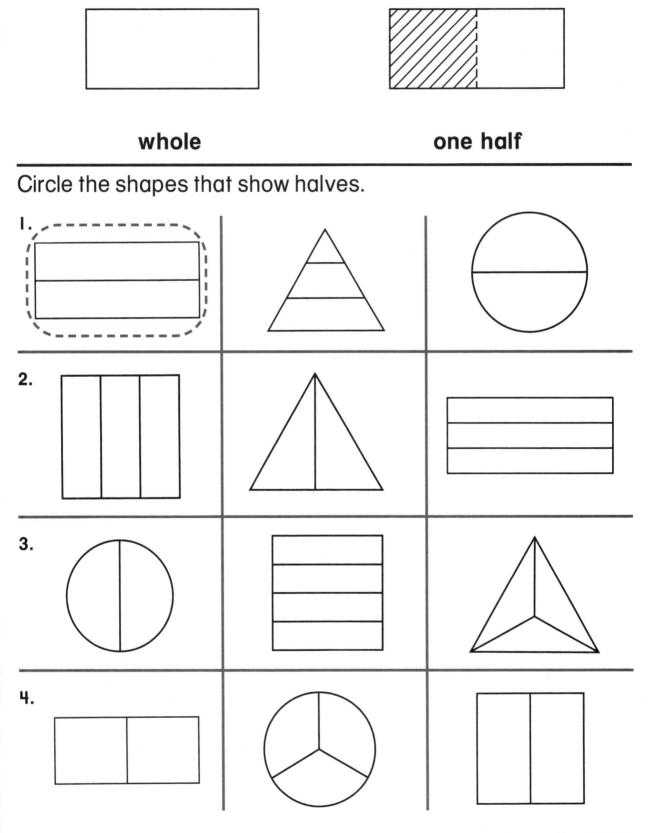

whole · · · · · · · · · · · · · · · one half

Circle the shapes that show halves.

Fourths

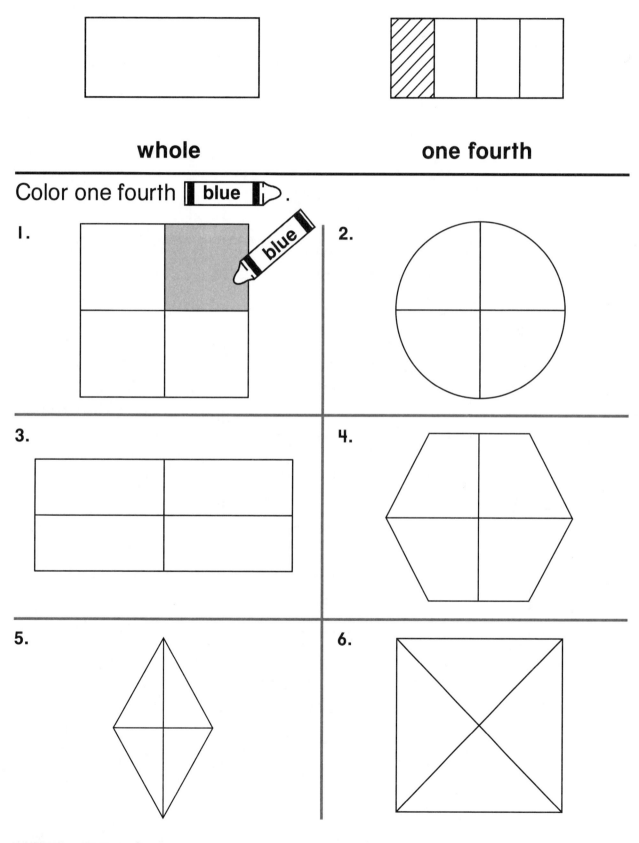

whole   **one fourth**

Color one fourth ▮ blue ▮⬡ .

1.

2.

3.

4.

5.

6.

Name _____

Thirds

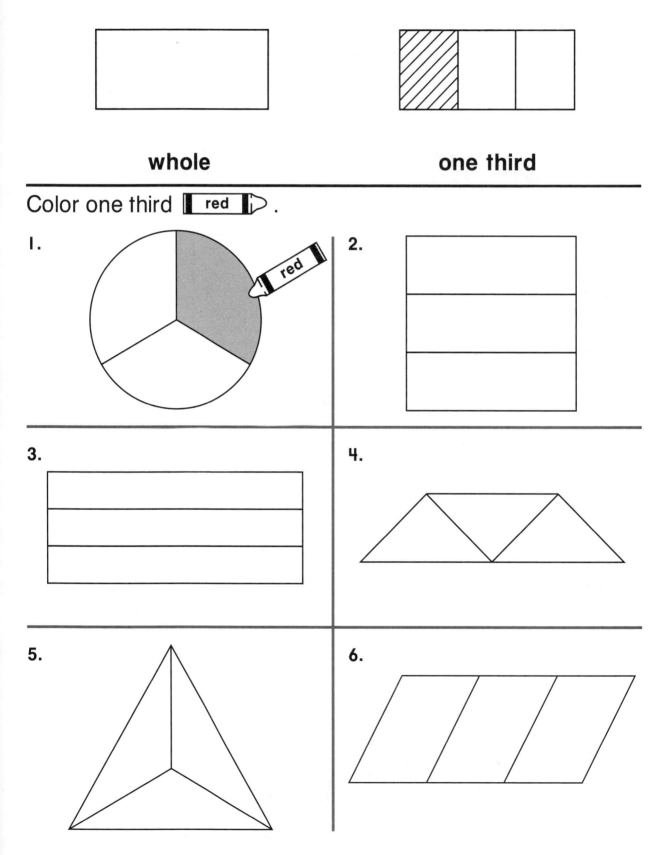

whole   **one third**

Color one third red .

1.

2.

3.

4.

5.

6.

Problem Solving • Use Logical Reasoning

Some children want to share sandwiches.
Use clues to solve.

1. Is the sandwich cut
   into 3 equal parts?

   No . It is cut into

   4 equal parts.

2. Is the sandwich cut
   into 3 equal parts?

   _____. It is cut into

   _____ equal parts.

3. Is the sandwich cut
   into 4 equal parts?

   _____. It is cut into

   _____ equal parts.

4. Is the sandwich cut
   into 4 equal parts?

   _____. It is cut into

   _____ equal parts.

Parts of Groups

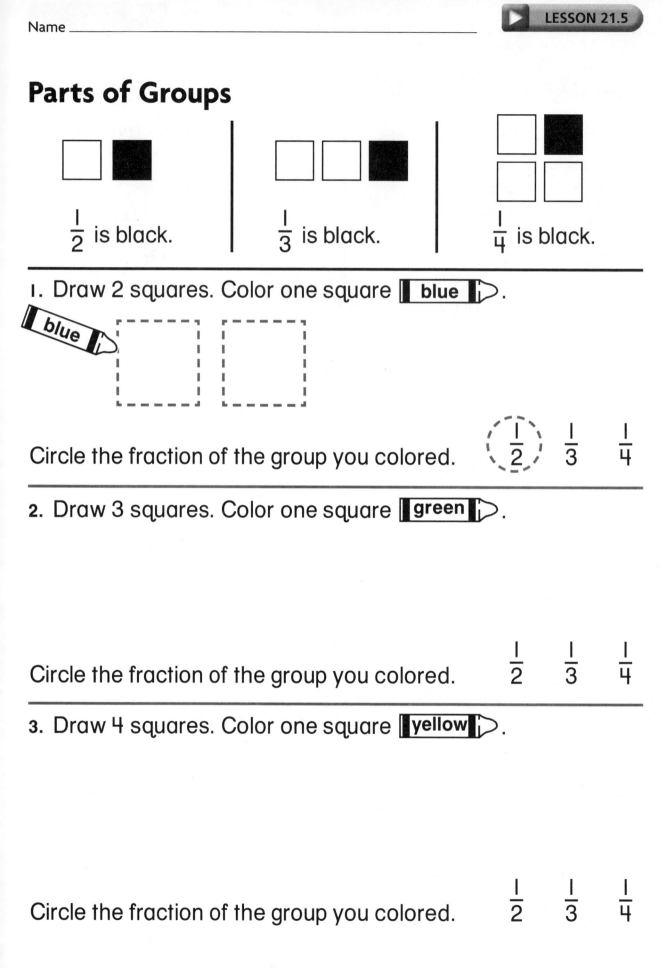

$\frac{1}{2}$ is black. $\frac{1}{3}$ is black. $\frac{1}{4}$ is black.

1. Draw 2 squares. Color one square **blue**.

Circle the fraction of the group you colored. $\frac{1}{2}$ $\frac{1}{3}$ $\frac{1}{4}$

2. Draw 3 squares. Color one square **green**.

Circle the fraction of the group you colored. $\frac{1}{2}$ $\frac{1}{3}$ $\frac{1}{4}$

3. Draw 4 squares. Color one square **yellow**.

Circle the fraction of the group you colored. $\frac{1}{2}$ $\frac{1}{3}$ $\frac{1}{4}$

Pennies and Nickels

Count pennies by ones.	Count nickels by fives.

1¢, 2¢	5¢, 10¢

Use pennies to show the amount.
Draw the coins.

1.
4¢   ⬭1¢ ⬭1¢ ⬭1¢ ⬭1¢

2.
5¢

3.
6¢

Use nickels to show the amount. Draw the coins.

4.
10¢

5.
15¢

Pennies and Dimes

Count dimes by tens.

10¢,　　　20¢,　　　30¢,　　　40¢

Use dimes to show the amount.
Draw the coins.

1. 10¢	10¢
2. 40¢	
3. 20¢	
4. 50¢	
5. 30¢	

Count Groups of Coins

Count by fives. Then count on by ones.

5¢,   10¢,   11¢,   12¢,   13¢   13¢

Count by tens. Then count on by ones.

10¢,   20¢,   21¢,   22¢   22¢

Count the coins. Circle the amount.

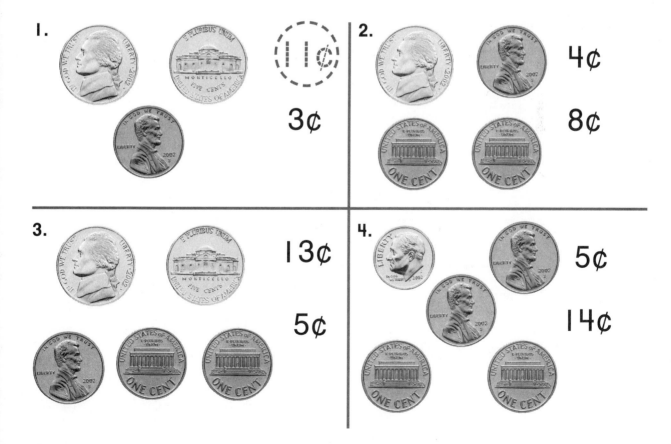

1.

11¢

3¢

2.

4¢

8¢

3.

13¢

5¢

4.

5¢

14¢

Name _____

Count Collections

Circle the coins that total 40¢.

1.

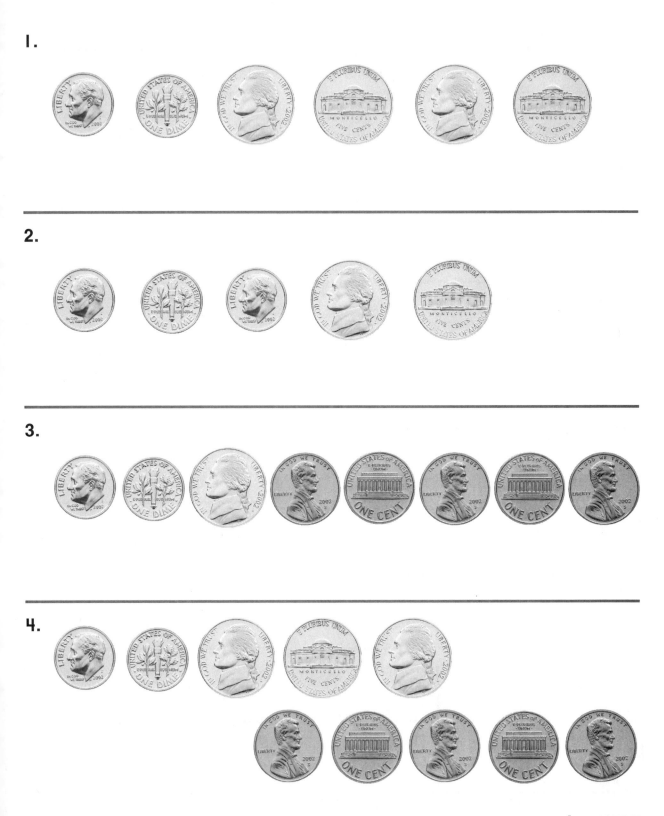

2.

3.

4.

Problem Solving • Make a List

Each row shows one way to make 20¢.
Write the missing numbers.

Ways to Make 20¢		
Dimes	**Nickels**	**Pennies**
2	0	0
1	1	5
1		0
	0	10
0	4	
0		5
0	2	
0		15
		20

Trade Pennies, Nickels, and Dimes

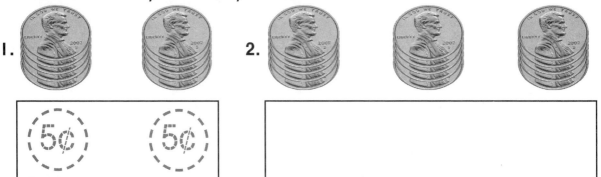

5 pennies = 1 nickel

10 pennies = 1 dime

Trade pennies for nickels.
Draw how many nickels you have.

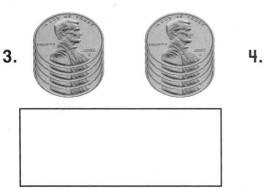

1.

(5¢) (5¢)

2.

Trade pennies for dimes.
Draw how many dimes you have.

3.

4.

Quarters

Count 25¢ for the quarter. Then count on.

25¢,   35¢   25¢,   30¢   25¢,   26¢

Count on from a quarter. Circle the amount.

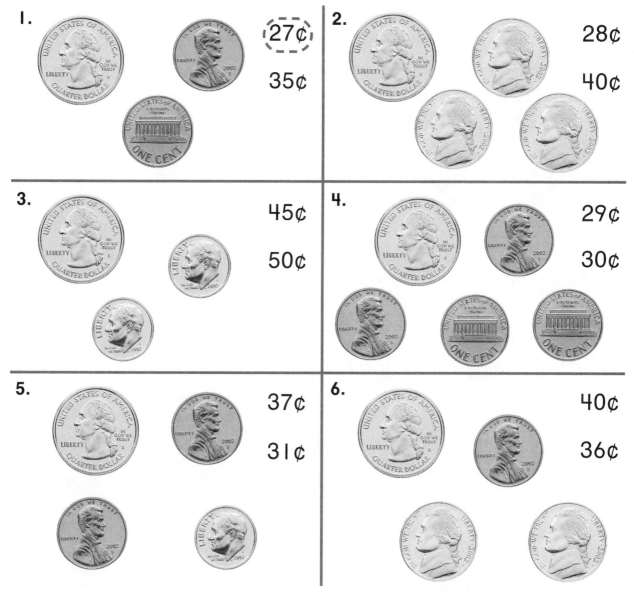

1.   (27¢)
      35¢

2.   28¢
      40¢

3.   45¢
      50¢

4.   29¢
      30¢

5.   37¢
      31¢

6.   40¢
      36¢

Half Dollar and Dollar

25¢,   50¢,   75¢,   100¢

Count by 25 to 100.

Count. Write the numbers. Circle the amount.

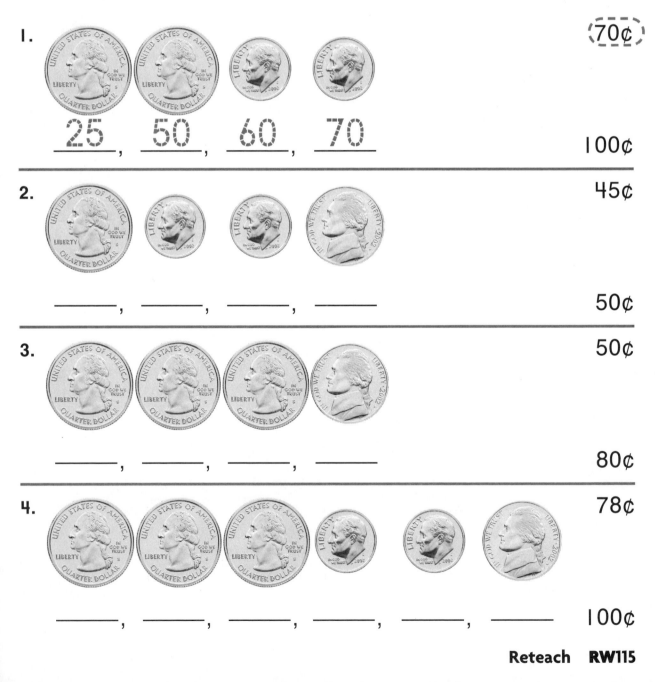

1.

$\underline{25}$, $\underline{50}$, $\underline{60}$, $\underline{70}$

(70¢)

100¢

2.

____, ____, ____, ____

45¢

50¢

3.

____, ____, ____, ____

50¢

80¢

4.

____, ____, ____, ____, ____, ____

78¢

100¢

Compare Values

Count each group of coins.
Circle the amount that is less.

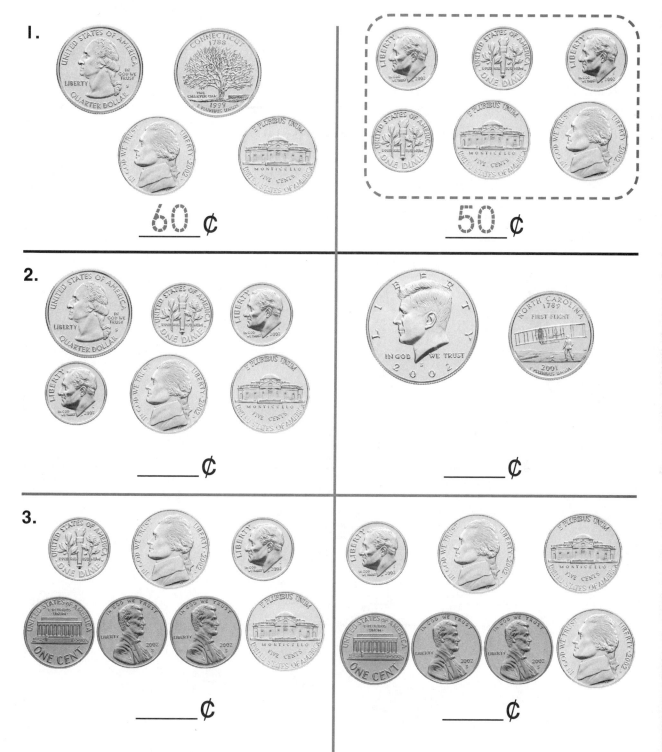

1.

60 ¢

50 ¢

2.

_____ ¢

_____ ¢

3.

_____ ¢

_____ ¢

Same Amounts

Count. Write the amount. Then use fewer
coins to show the same amount.

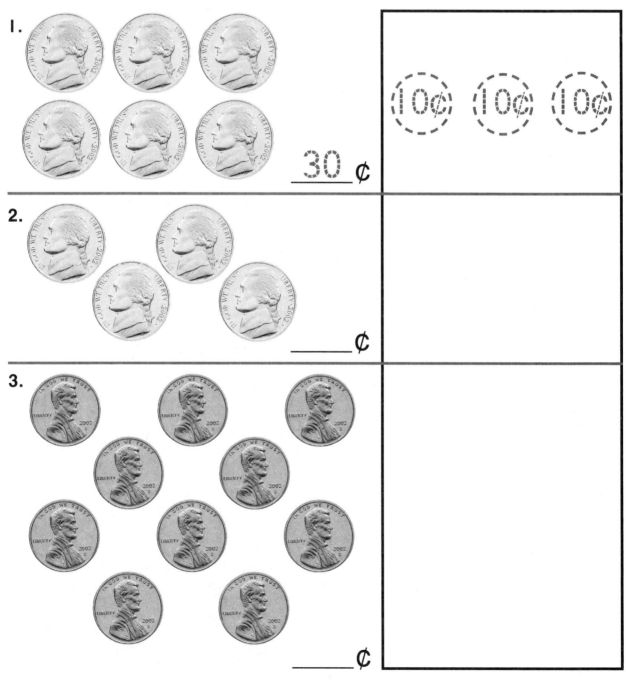

1.

_30_ ¢

10¢   10¢   10¢

2.

_____ ¢

3.

_____ ¢

Problem Solving • Act It Out

Use the fewest coins to show the same amount.
Draw them in the empty pocket.

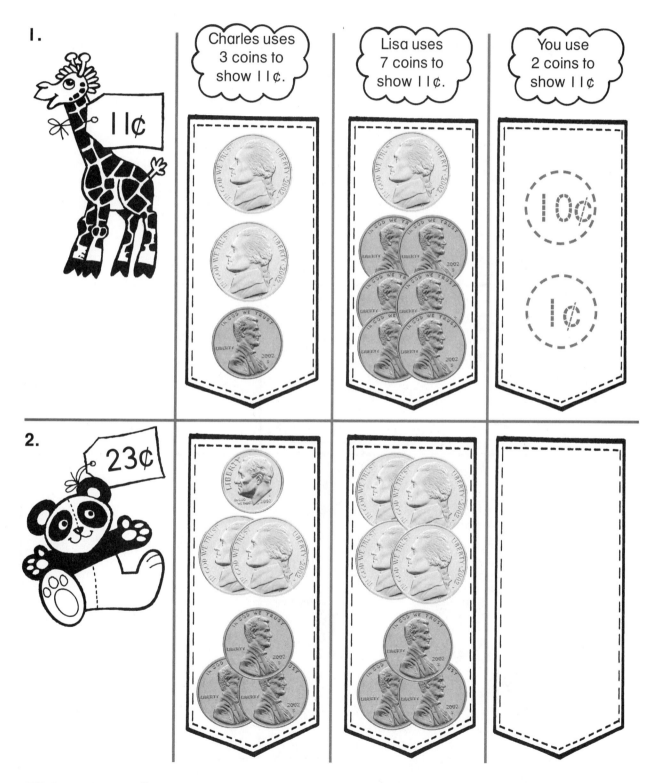

1.

11¢

Charles uses 3 coins to show 11¢.

Lisa uses 7 coins to show 11¢.

You use 2 coins to show 11¢

10¢

1¢

2.

23¢

Read a Clock

Use a 🕐 . Show each time.
Complete the sentences. Circle the time.

1.

The hour hand points to ___5___ .

The minute hand points to ___12___ .

(**5 o'clock**)   6 o'clock

2.

The hour hand points to ____ .

The minute hand points to ____ .

9 o'clock   1 o'clock

3.

The hour hand points to ____ .

The minute hand points to ____ .

10 o'clock   2 o'clock

4.

The hour hand points to ____ .

The minute hand points to ____ .

12 o'clock   7 o'clock

Problem Solving • Use Estimation

counting 100 pennies
more than a minute

counting 5 pennies
less than a minute

Circle the one that would take **more than a minute**. Act it out.

1.

2.

Circle the one that would take **less than a minute**. Act it out.

3.

Time to the Hour

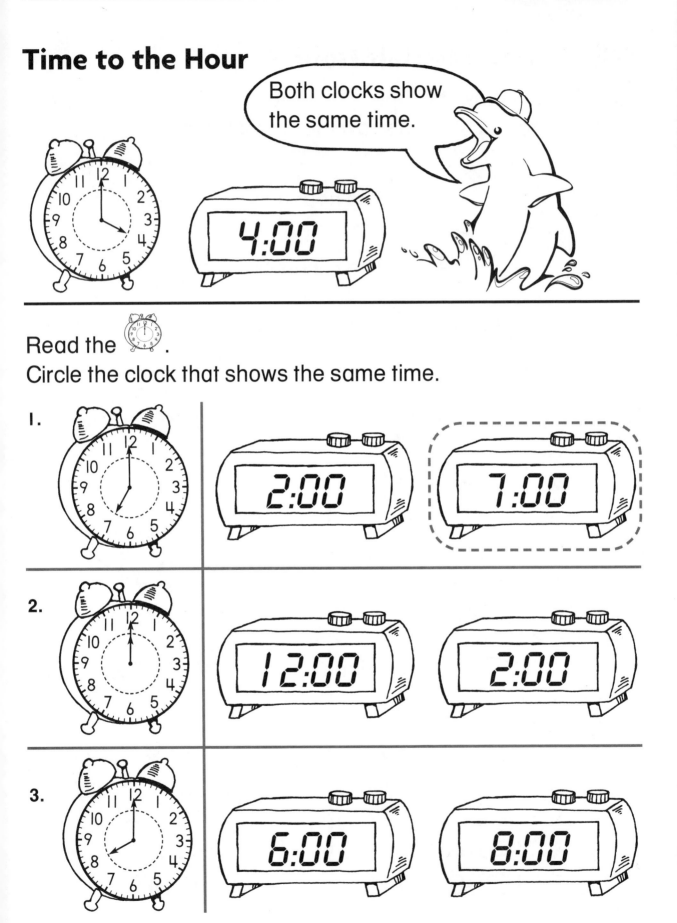

Both clocks show the same time.

Read the 🕐.

Circle the clock that shows the same time.

1.

2:00   7:00

2.

12:00   2:00

3.

6:00   8:00

Tell Time to the Half Hour

Use a clock. Show the time.
Draw the minute hand to show the correct time.

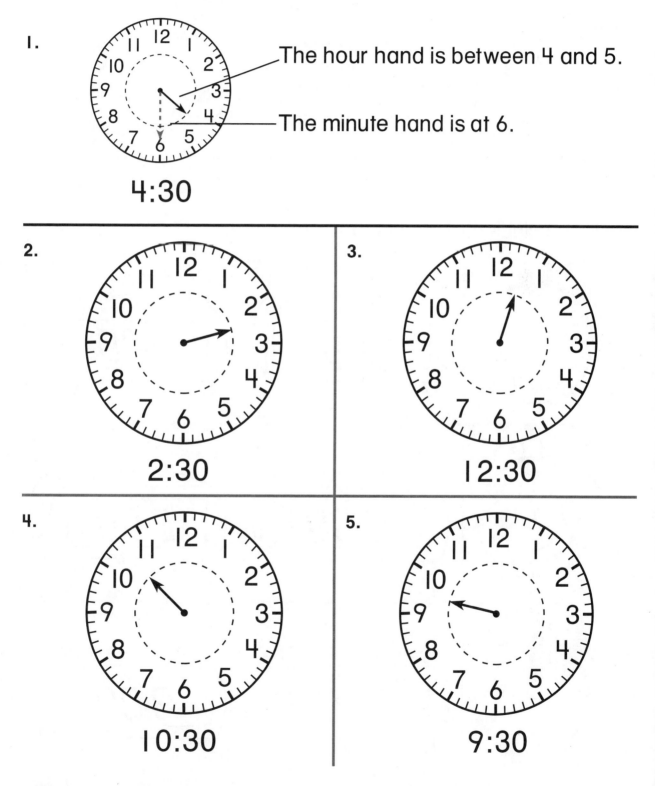

1.

The hour hand is between 4 and 5.

The minute hand is at 6.

4:30

2.

2:30

3.

12:30

4.

10:30

5.

9:30

Practice Time to the Hour and Half Hour

Use a clock. Show the time.
Draw the hour hand and the minute hand.

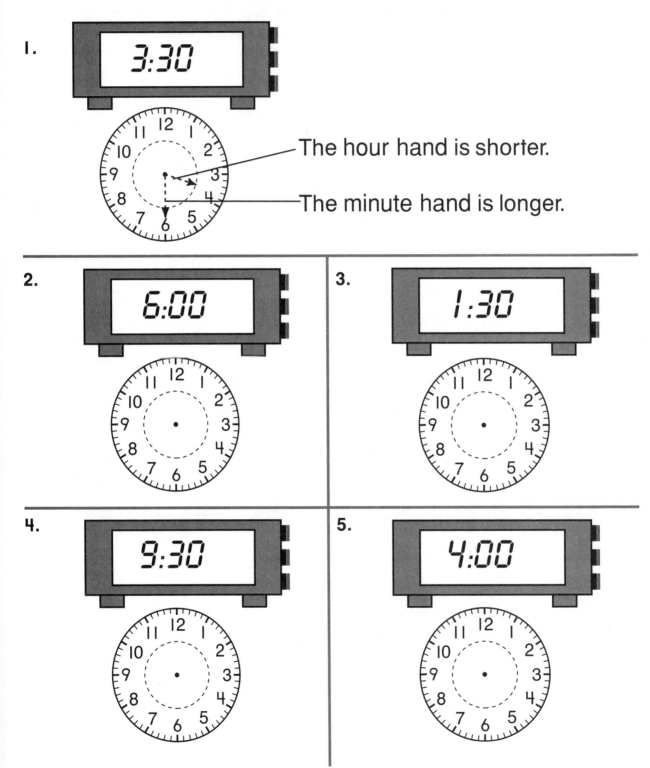

1. 3:30

The hour hand is shorter.

The minute hand is longer.

2. 6:00

3. 1:30

4. 9:30

5. 4:00

Use a Calendar

January	February	March	April	May	June

July	August	September	October	November	December

Circle the next month.

1. February, March, April,   (May)

                                                              June

2. September, October, November,   December

                                                              July

3. June, July, August,   February

                                                              September

4. January, February, March,   April

                                                              October

Sunday	Monday	Tuesday	Wednesday	Thursday	Friday	Saturday

Circle the next day.

5. Sunday, Monday, Tuesday,   Friday

                                                              Wednesday

6. Wednesday, Thursday, Friday,   Saturday

                                                              Monday

Daily Events

1. Draw a picture to show something you do in the morning.

2. Draw a picture to show something you do in the afternoon.

3. Draw a picture to show something you do in the evening.

Problem Solving • Make a Graph

Some children talked about which meal they like best.
Then they made a picture graph.

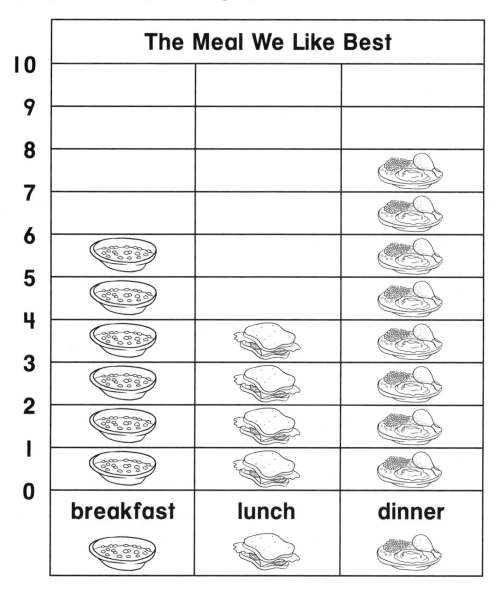

Use the graph to answer the questions.

1. How many children like breakfast best? _____

2. How many children like lunch best? _____

3. How many more children chose dinner than lunch? _____

4. How many children chose breakfast or lunch? _____

Name _____

Read a Schedule

Start	End
9:00	9:30

half an hour

Start	End
9:30	10:00

half an hour

Start	End
9:00	10:00

one hour

Use the chart. Circle the answers.

At the Lake	Start	End
Swim	5:00	6:00
Games	6:00	6:30
Dinner	6:30	7:00
Songs	7:00	8:00

1. Which activity comes after dinner?   Games

    (Songs)

2. Which activity comes before games?   Swim

    Dinner

3. How long does dinner last?   One hour

    Half an hour

4. How long does swimming last?   One hour

    Half an hour

Problem Solving • Make Reasonable Estimates

Which activity takes about 1 hour?

This takes about 1 minute.   This takes about 1 hour.

Circle the activity that takes about 1 hour.

1.

2.

3.

Compare Lengths

Compare lengths.

Color the longest object ▌ red ▷.

Color the shortest object ▌ blue ▷.

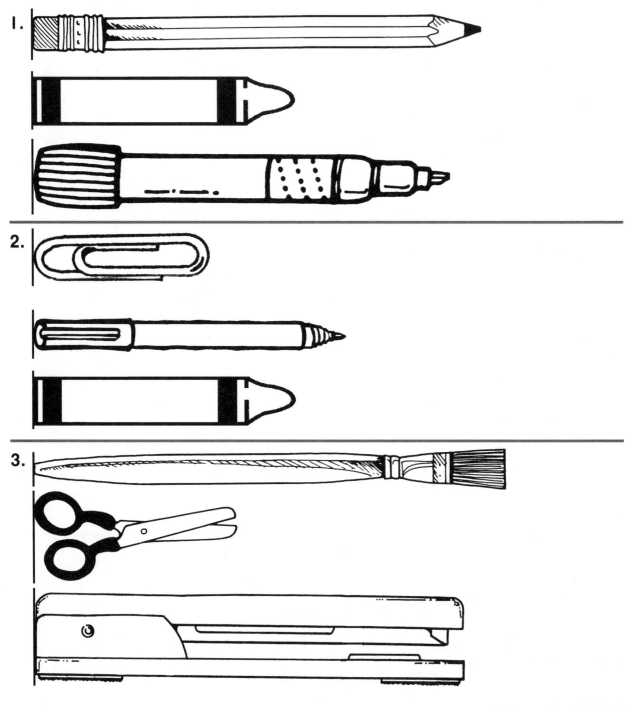

Use Nonstandard Units

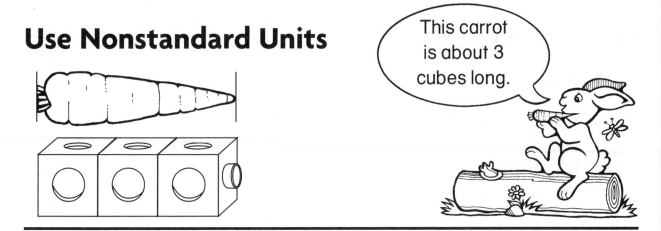

This carrot is about 3 cubes long.

About how long is it? Use 🎲 to measure.

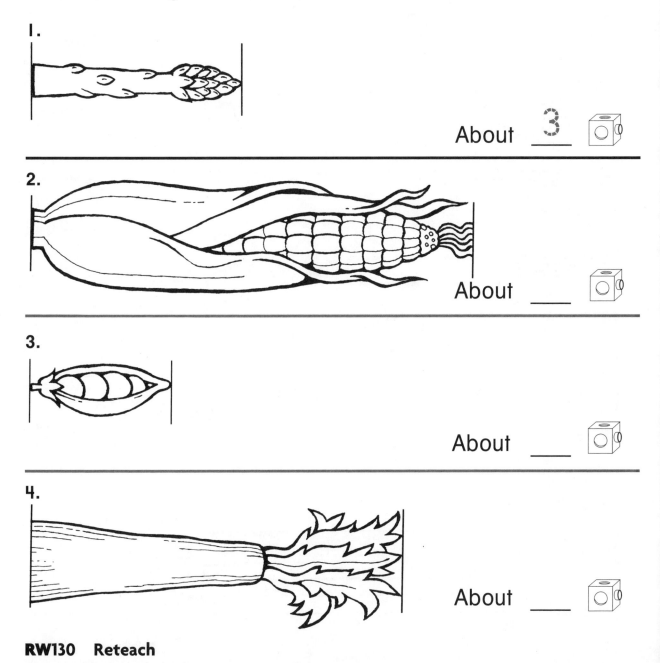

1.

About ___3___ 🎲

2.

About ___ 🎲

3.

About ___ 🎲

4.

About ___ 🎲

Name _____

Inches

Use an inch ruler to measure. Circle how many inches.

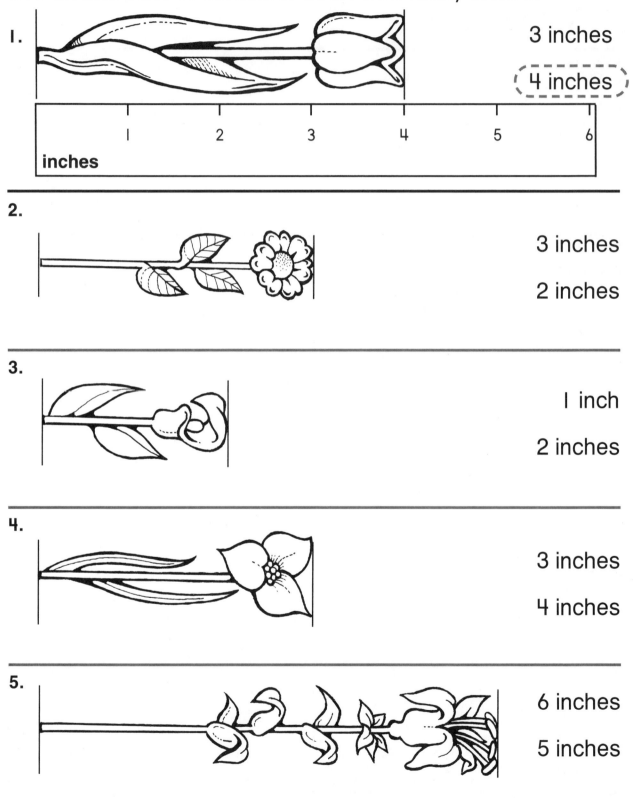

1. 3 inches

   (4 inches)

2. 3 inches

   2 inches

3. 1 inch

   2 inches

4. 3 inches

   4 inches

5. 6 inches

   5 inches

Inches and Feet

Choose the unit you would use to measure.
Circle **inches** or **feet**.

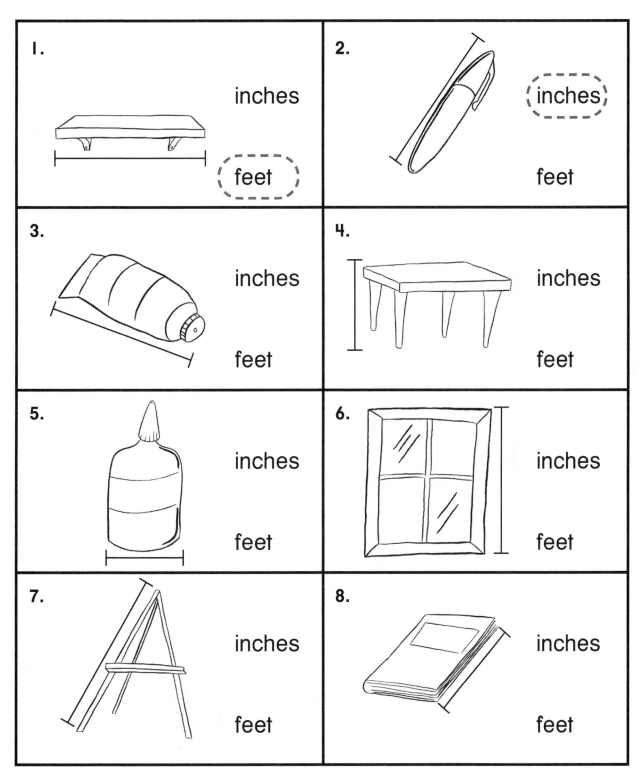

1. inches

    (feet)

2. (inches)

    feet

3. inches

    feet

4. inches

    feet

5. inches

    feet

6. inches

    feet

7. inches

    feet

8. inches

    feet

Centimeters

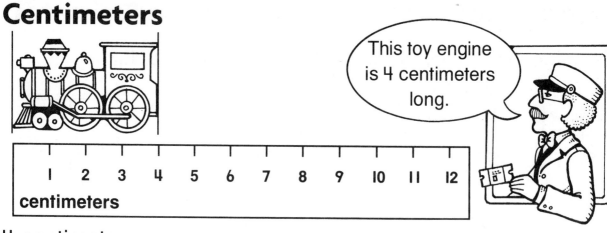

This toy engine is 4 centimeters long.

1	2	3	4	5	6	7	8	9	10	11	12

centimeters

4 centimeters

Use a centimeter ruler. Measure.
Circle how many centimeters.

1.

6 centimeters

4 centimeters

(8 centimeters)

2.

10 centimeters

7 centimeters

5 centimeters

3.

14 centimeters

12 centimeters

10 centimeters

Problem Solving • Make Reasonable Estimates

Estimate how many train cars will fit on each track.

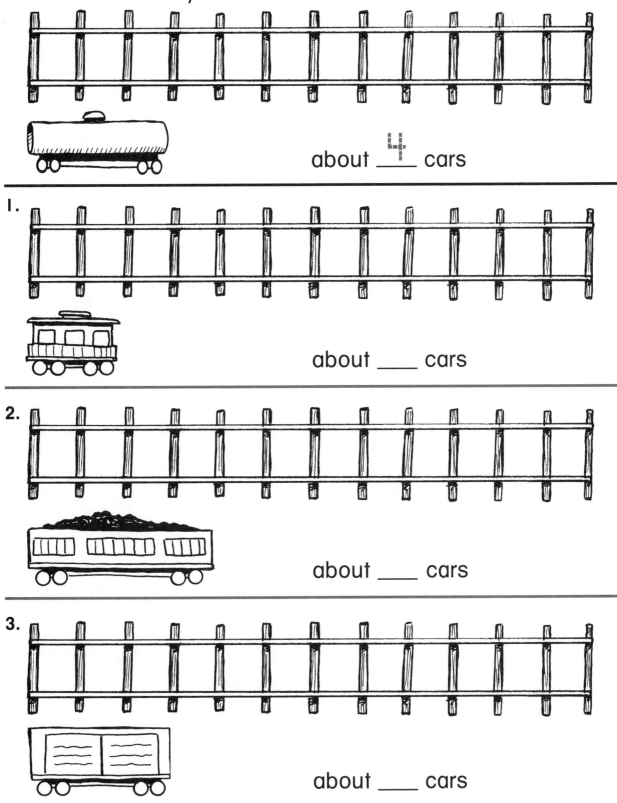

about __4__ cars

1. about ____ cars

2. about ____ cars

3. about ____ cars

Use a Balance

Balance each object with 🎲.

Draw how many 🎲 you use.

1.

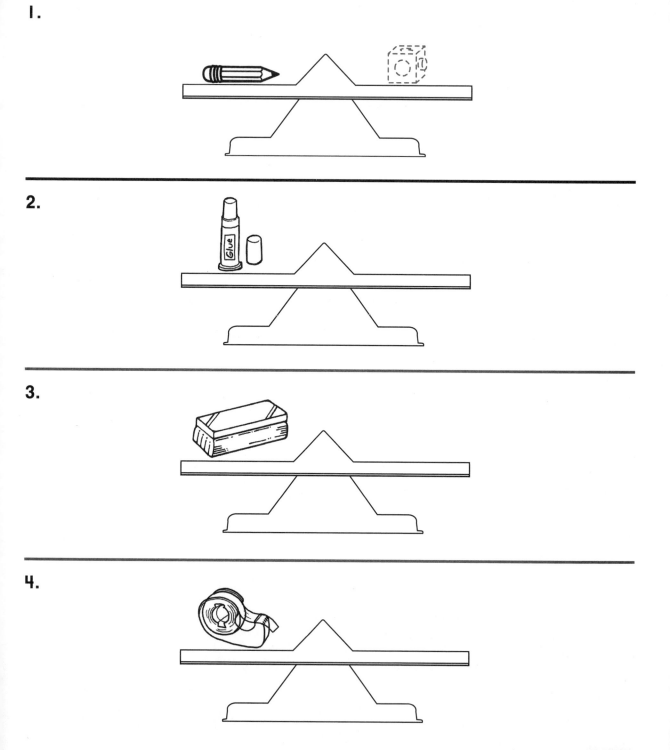

2.

3.

4.

Pounds

Look at each object.
Write 1 or 10 to show the better estimate.

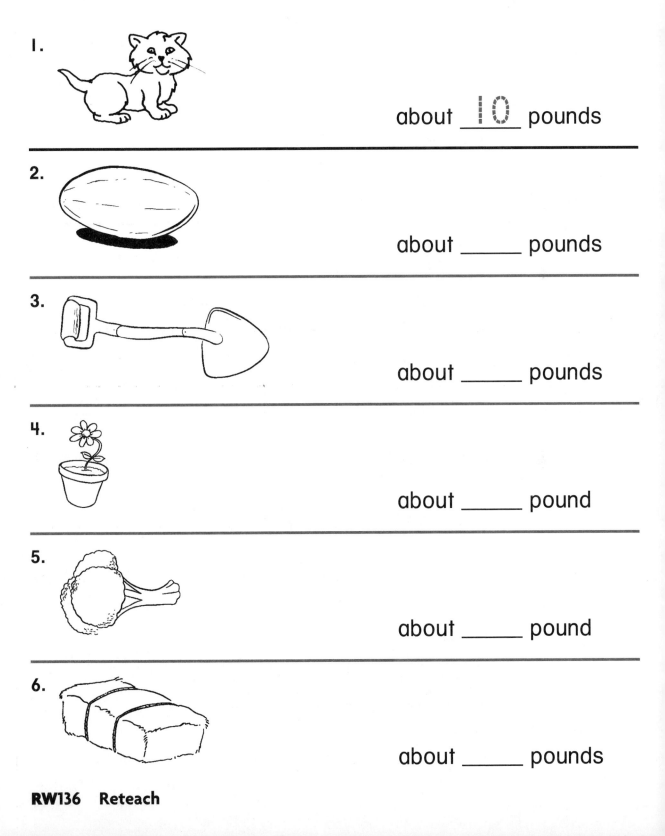

1.

about __10__ pounds

2.

about _____ pounds

3.

about _____ pounds

4.

about _____ pound

5.

about _____ pound

6.

about _____ pounds

Kilograms

Look at each object.
Circle grams or kilograms.

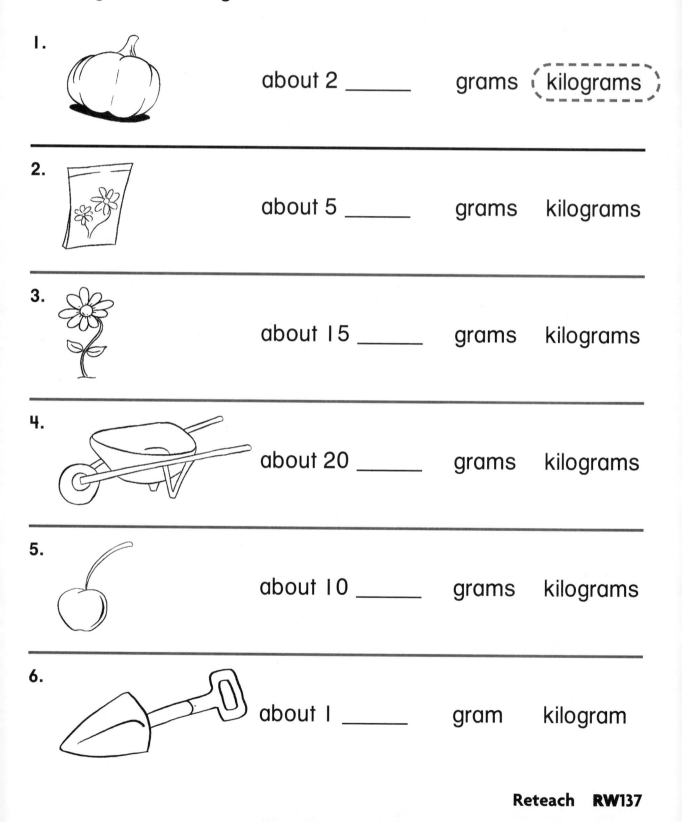

1.

about 2 _____   grams   (kilograms)

2.

about 5 _____   grams   kilograms

3.

about 15 _____   grams   kilograms

4.

about 20 _____   grams   kilograms

5.

about 10 _____   grams   kilograms

6.

about 1 _____   gram   kilogram

Problem Solving • Predict and Test

Predict how many paper clips to balance.
Draw the paper clips.
Measure. Draw how many paper clips to balance.

1. **Predict**   **Test**

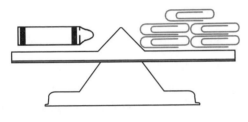   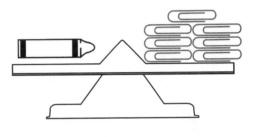

2. **Predict**   **Test**

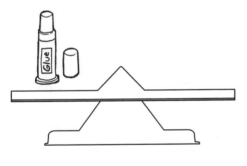

3. **Predict**   **Test**

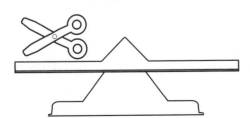   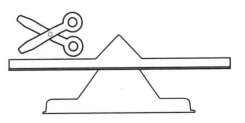

Name _____

Nonstandard Units

Match the container with the units.

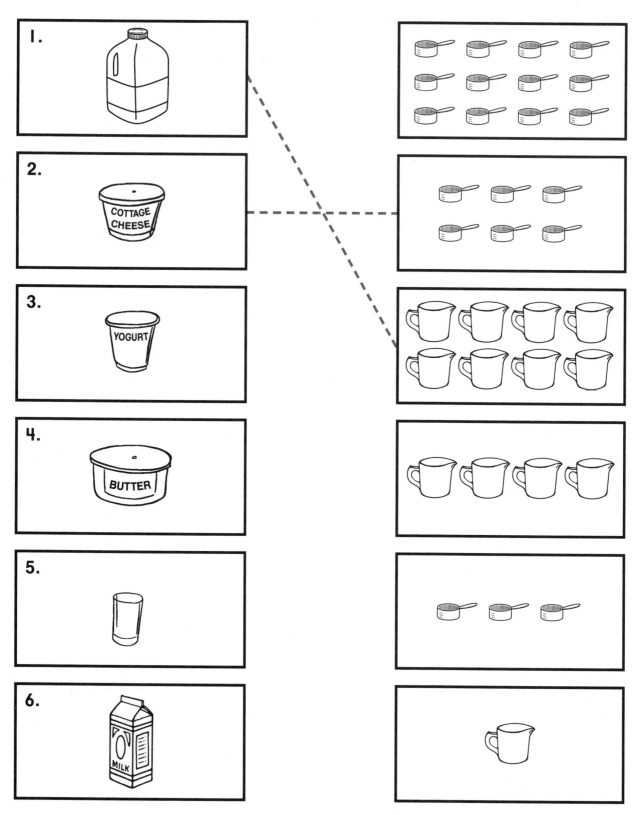

Cups, Pints, Quarts

Estimate. Then use 🥛 to measure.

Color 🥛 to show how much the container holds.

Container	Estimate	Measurement
1.	about __2__ cups	
2.	about ____ cup	
3.	about ____ cups	
4.	about ____ cups	
5.	about ____ cups	
6.	about ____ cup	

Liters

Circle the closer estimate.

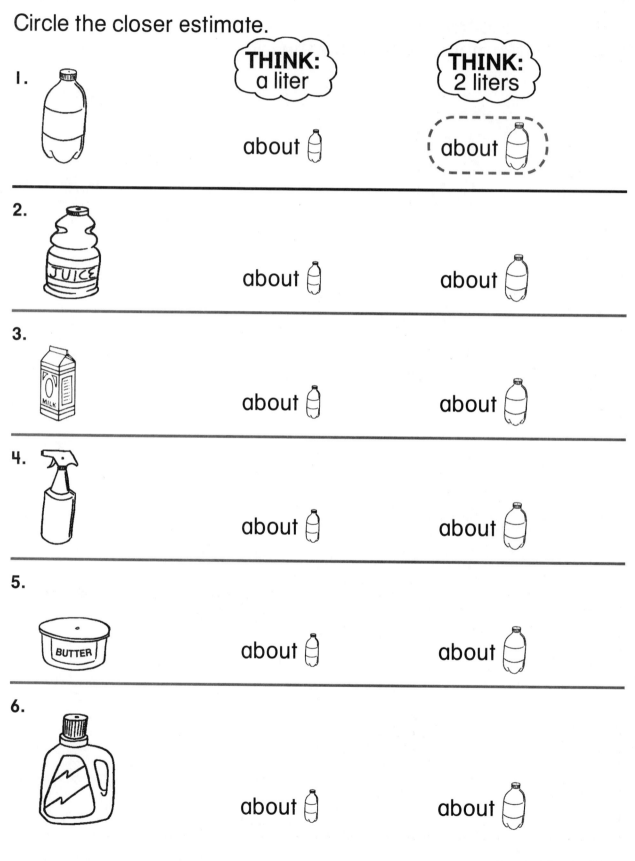

1.
THINK: a liter
about 🍶

THINK: 2 liters
about 🍾

2.
about 🍶
about 🍾

3.
about 🍶
about 🍾

4.
about 🍶
about 🍾

5.
about 🍶
about 🍾

6.
about 🍶
about 🍾

Name _____

Temperature

Circle the temperature.
Color the thermometer to show the temperature.

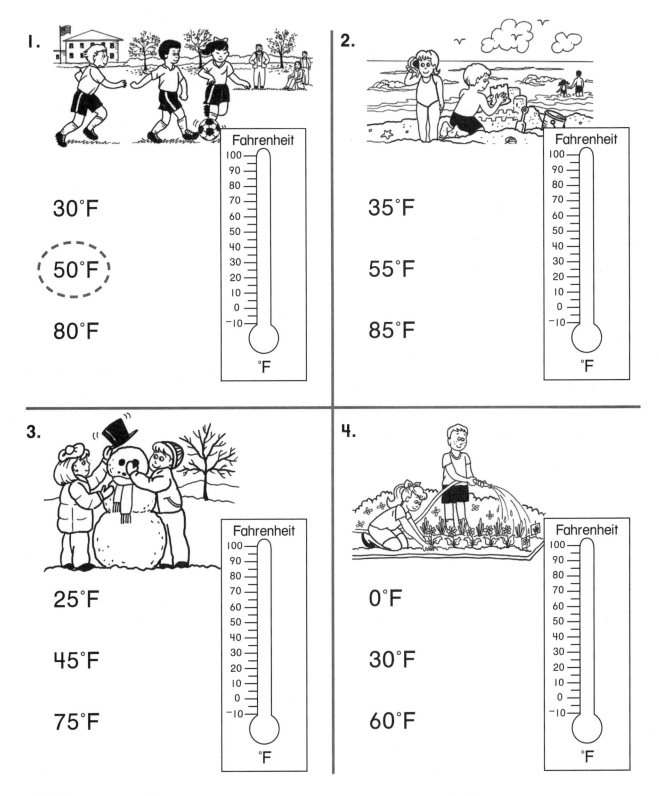

1. 30°F (50°F) 80°F

2. 35°F 55°F 85°F

3. 25°F 45°F 75°F

4. 0°F 30°F 60°F

RW142   Reteach

Problem Solving • Choose the Measuring Tool

Look at the pictures.

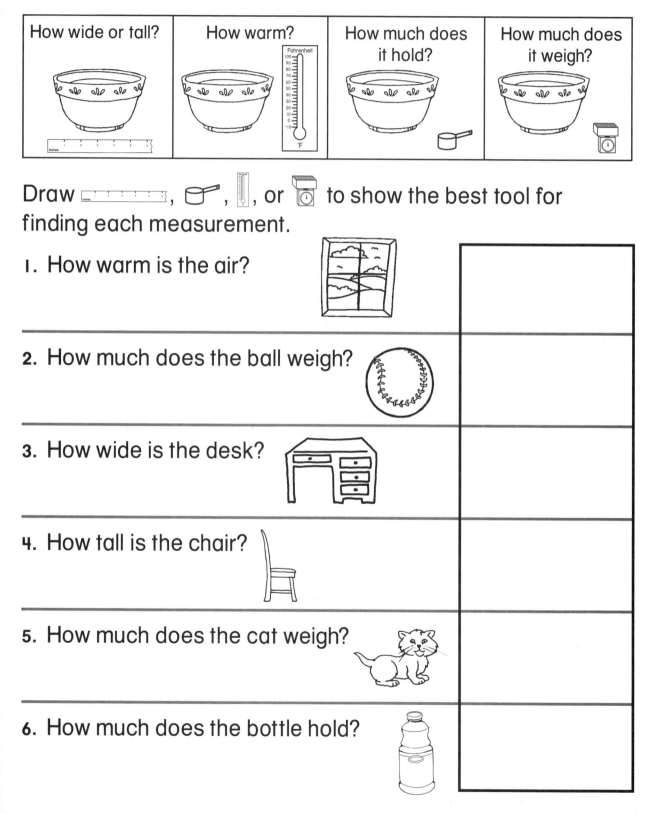

| How wide or tall? | How warm? | How much does it hold? | How much does it weigh? |

Draw [ruler], [measuring cup], [thermometer], or [scale] to show the best tool for finding each measurement.

1. How warm is the air?

2. How much does the ball weigh?

3. How wide is the desk?

4. How tall is the chair?

5. How much does the cat weigh?

6. How much does the bottle hold?

Name

Use Mental Math to Add Tens

Add.

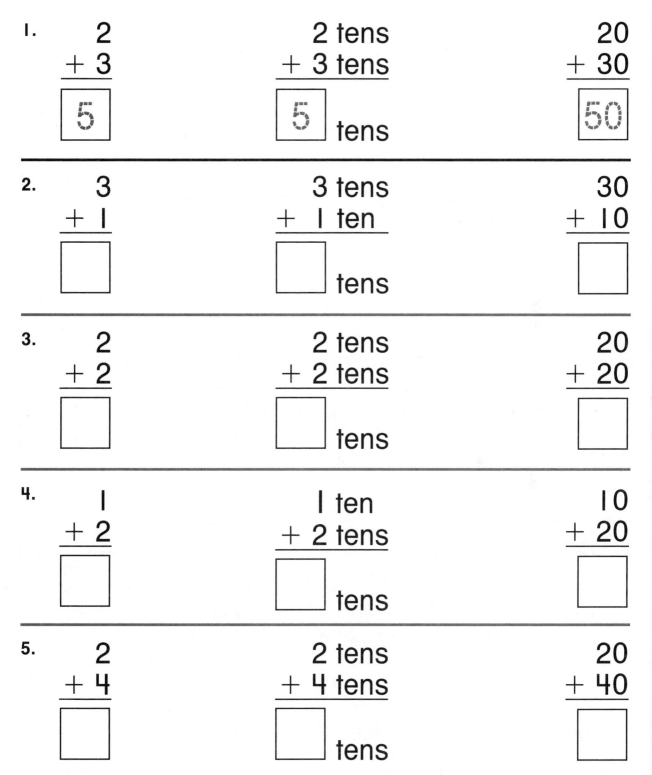

1.
```
    2          2 tens          20
  + 3        + 3 tens        + 30
  ┌───┐      ┌───┐           ┌────┐
  │ 5 │      │ 5 │ tens      │ 50 │
  └───┘      └───┘           └────┘
```

2.
```
    3          3 tens          30
  + 1        + 1 ten         + 10
  ┌───┐      ┌───┐           ┌────┐
  │   │      │   │ tens      │    │
  └───┘      └───┘           └────┘
```

3.
```
    2          2 tens          20
  + 2        + 2 tens        + 20
  ┌───┐      ┌───┐           ┌────┐
  │   │      │   │ tens      │    │
  └───┘      └───┘           └────┘
```

4.
```
    1          1 ten           10
  + 2        + 2 tens        + 20
  ┌───┐      ┌───┐           ┌────┐
  │   │      │   │ tens      │    │
  └───┘      └───┘           └────┘
```

5.
```
    2          2 tens          20
  + 4        + 4 tens        + 40
  ┌───┐      ┌───┐           ┌────┐
  │   │      │   │ tens      │    │
  └───┘      └───┘           └────┘
```

Add Tens and Ones

Use the pictures to add. Circle all the ones.
Complete the number sentence.

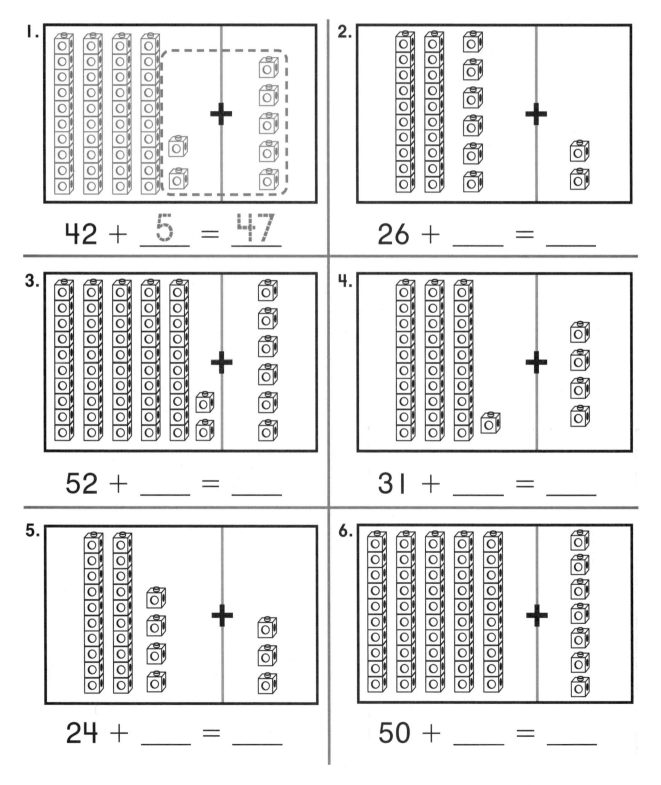

1. $42 + \underline{5} = \underline{47}$

2. $26 + \underline{} = \underline{}$

3. $52 + \underline{} = \underline{}$

4. $31 + \underline{} = \underline{}$

5. $24 + \underline{} = \underline{}$

6. $50 + \underline{} = \underline{}$

Name _____

Add Money

Write the amounts the coins show.
Add.

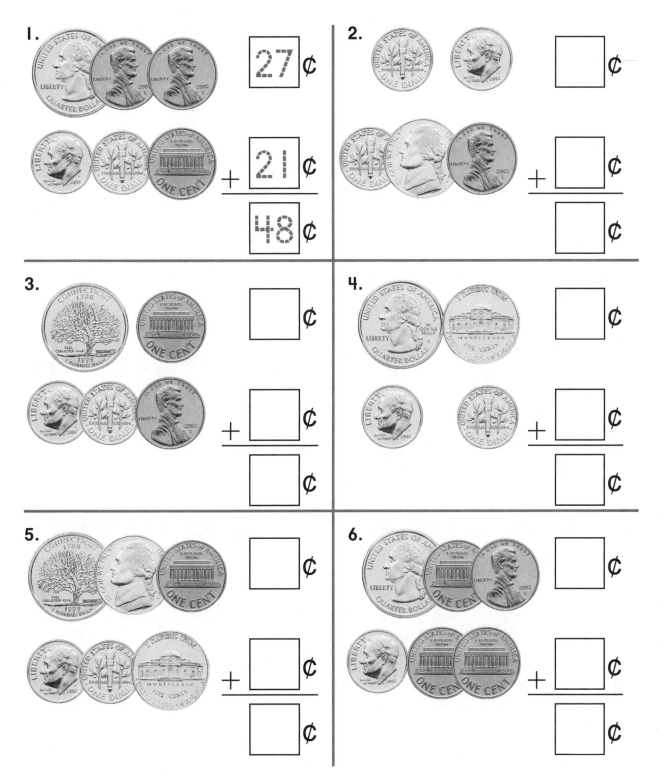

1. 27 ¢
    + 21 ¢
    48 ¢

2. ☐ ¢
    + ☐ ¢
    ☐ ¢

3. ☐ ¢
    + ☐ ¢
    ☐ ¢

4. ☐ ¢
    + ☐ ¢
    ☐ ¢

5. ☐ ¢
    + ☐ ¢
    ☐ ¢

6. ☐ ¢
    + ☐ ¢
    ☐ ¢

Use Mental Math to Subtract Tens

Subtract tens. Write the numbers. Count back
and cross out tens to check. Circle the answer.

1. 5 tens   50
    − 3 tens   − 30

    [2] tens   [20]

    10, (20), 30, 40, 50

    Subtract
    3 tens.
    You have
    20 left.

2. 6 tens   60
    − 2 tens   − 20

    [ ] tens   [ ]

    10, 20, 30, 40, 50, 60

3. 4 tens   40
    − 1 ten   − 10

    [ ] tens   [ ]

    10, 20, 30, 40

4. 7 tens   70
    − 2 tens   − 20

    [ ] tens   [ ]

    10, 20, 30, 40, 50, 60, 70

5. 6 tens   60
    − 3 tens   − 30

    [ ] tens   [ ]

    10, 20, 30, 40, 50, 60

Name _____

Subtract Tens and Ones

Use the pictures. Cross out to show what you subtract.
Write the difference.

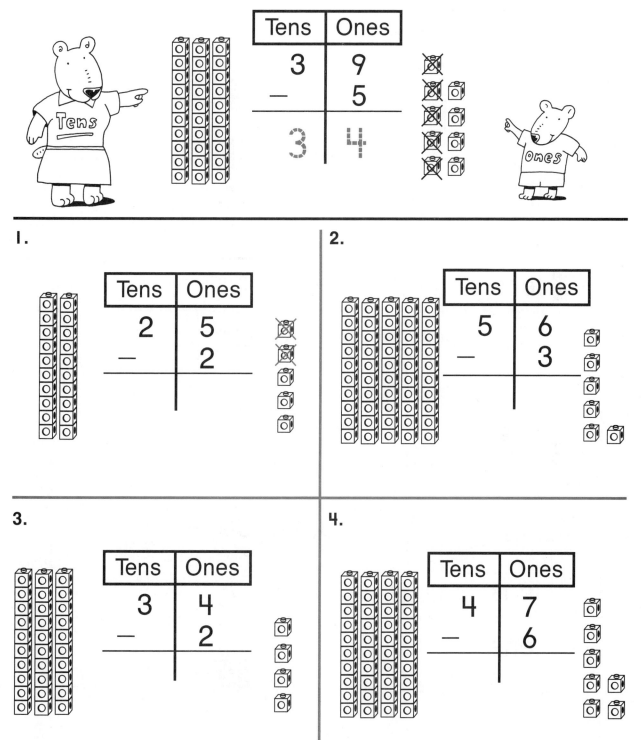

Tens	Ones
3	9
−	5
3	4

1.

Tens	Ones
2	5
−	2

2.

Tens	Ones
5	6
−	3

3.

Tens	Ones
3	4
−	2

4.

Tens	Ones
4	7
−	6

Subtract Money

Write the amounts the coins show.
Subtract.

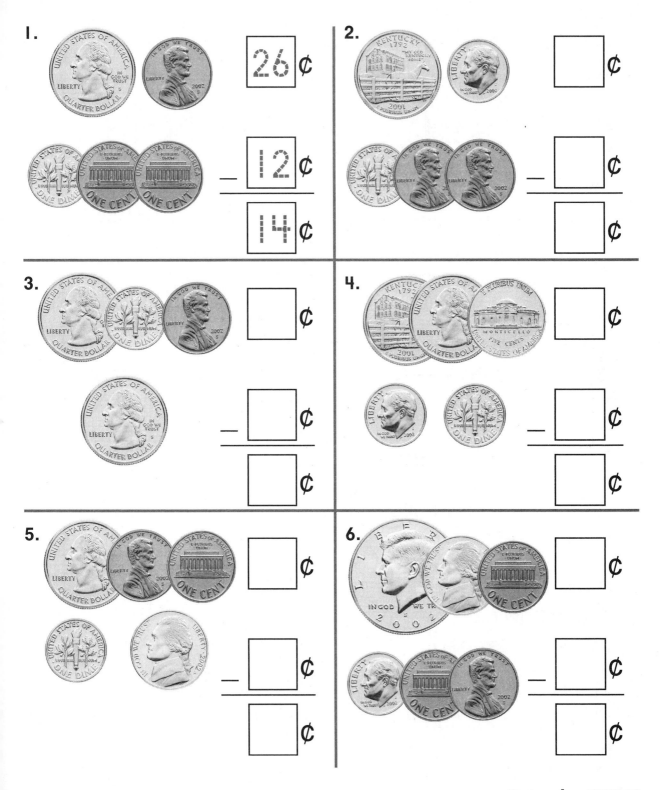

1.

$\begin{array}{r} 26 \cancel{c} \\ -\ 12 \cancel{c} \\ \hline 14 \cancel{c} \end{array}$

2.

$\begin{array}{r} \boxed{} \cancel{c} \\ -\ \boxed{} \cancel{c} \\ \hline \boxed{} \cancel{c} \end{array}$

3.

$\begin{array}{r} \boxed{} \cancel{c} \\ -\ \boxed{} \cancel{c} \\ \hline \boxed{} \cancel{c} \end{array}$

4.

$\begin{array}{r} \boxed{} \cancel{c} \\ -\ \boxed{} \cancel{c} \\ \hline \boxed{} \cancel{c} \end{array}$

5.

$\begin{array}{r} \boxed{} \cancel{c} \\ -\ \boxed{} \cancel{c} \\ \hline \boxed{} \cancel{c} \end{array}$

6.

$\begin{array}{r} \boxed{} \cancel{c} \\ -\ \boxed{} \cancel{c} \\ \hline \boxed{} \cancel{c} \end{array}$

Name _____

Problem Solving • Make Reasonable Estimates

Write 5, 30, 70, or 100.

1. There were 39 birds.
   12 flew away. About
   how many birds are left?   about _____ birds

2. There are 26 nuts.
   Joey eats 19 of the nuts.
   About how many nuts
   are left?   about _____ nuts

3. Rolf's backpack weighs
   22 pounds. Kyra's pack
   weighs 53 pounds.
   About how much do the
   packs weigh altogether?   about _____ pounds

4. Charlie took 28 pictures.
   Diego took 21 pictures.
   Rosa took 24 pictures.
   About how many pictures
   are there in all?   about _____ pictures

5. A toy car costs 48¢.
   About how much would
   two toy cars cost?   about _____ ¢

6. 78 children went on a trip.
   47 were boys. About
   how many were girls?   about _____ girls

Name _____

Certain or Impossible

Circle the bowls where it is certain to pull a cube.
Put an **X** on the bowls where it is impossible to pull a cube.

1.
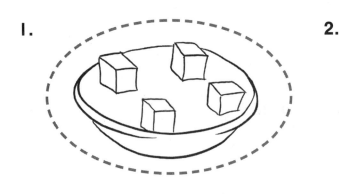

2.
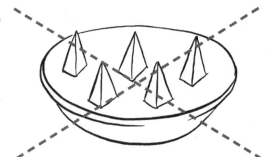

3.

4.
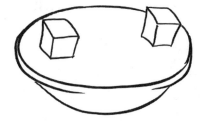

5.

6.
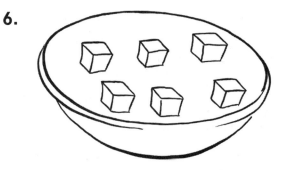

7.

8.
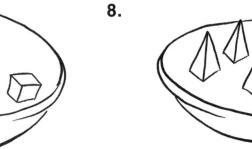

More Likely, Less Likely

Write how many circles and triangles.
Draw a ◯ or △ to show
which is more or less likely to pull.

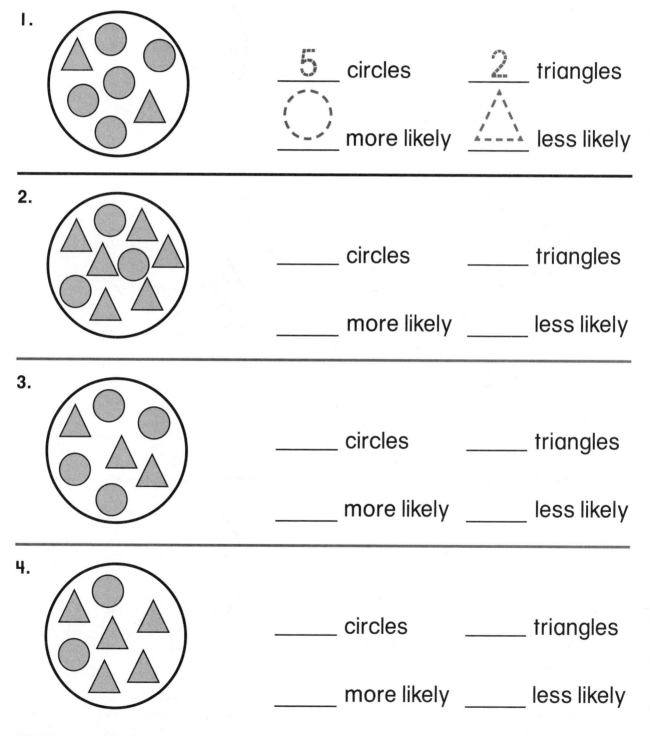

1.

_____5_____ circles   _____2_____ triangles

◯ more likely   △ less likely

2.

_____ circles   _____ triangles

_____ more likely   _____ less likely

3.

_____ circles   _____ triangles

_____ more likely   _____ less likely

4.

_____ circles   _____ triangles

_____ more likely   _____ less likely

Equally Likely

Draw a ☐, ○, or △
to show which are equally likely.

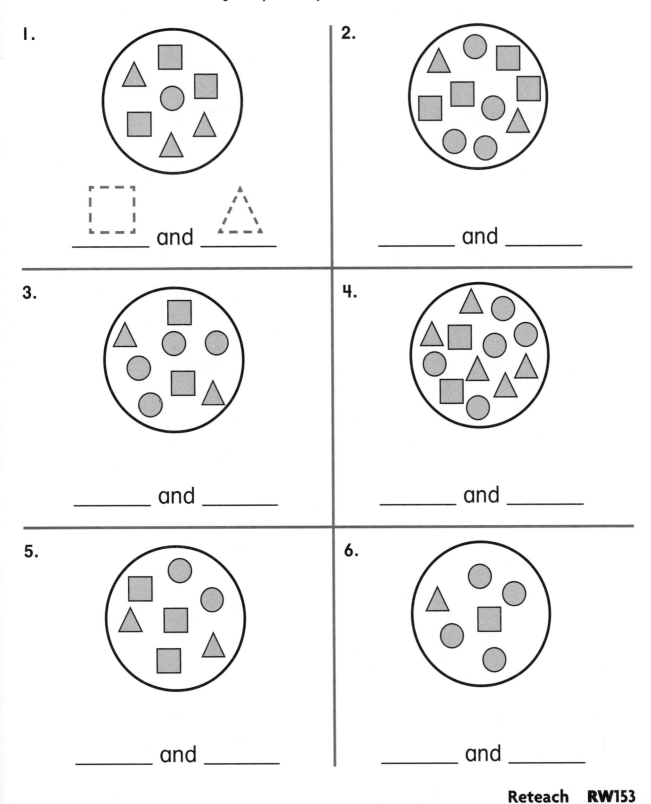

1.

_____ and _____

2.

_____ and _____

3.

_____ and _____

4.

_____ and _____

5.

_____ and _____

6.

_____ and _____

Problem Solving • Make a Prediction

If you spin the pointer 10 times, on which
number will it stop more often? Write the number.

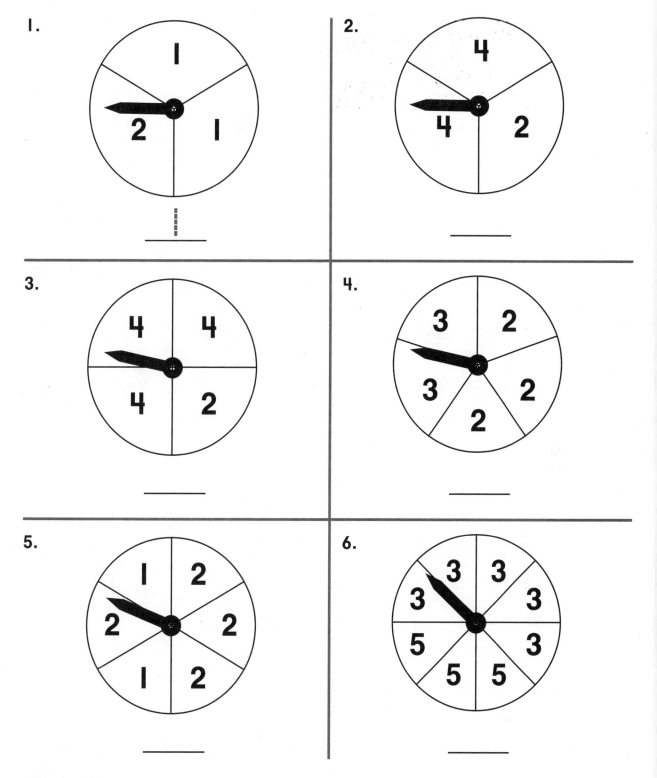

1.

2.

_____

3.

_____

4.

_____

5.

_____

6.

_____

HARCOURT

Edmund F. Lindop School
District 92
2400 South 18th Avenue
Broadview, IL 60155-3974

Reteach
Workbook

Grade 1

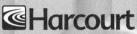

Orlando Austin Chicago New York Toronto London San Diego

Visit *The Learning Site!*
www.harcourtschool.com